Life Is Simple — First Cutting

Life Is Simple — First Cutting

By

Jerry Crownover

Published by Leathers Publishing
4500 College Blvd., Suite 310
Leawood, Kansas 66211
1/888/888-7696

Copyright 1998
Printed in the United States

ISBN: 1-890622-43-5

Cover sketch by Bill Green

This book is dedicated to the memory of a farmer and my father, Eugene Crownover. He was a man who knew there were only two ways to do something — the right way or the wrong way, two answers to any question — the truth or a lie, and only one way to be successful — work for it.

Ranch Dog

I FELT SORRY FOR HIM as I drove by early last Saturday morning. This cowboy, who runs cattle on a place just east of mine, was on his way to the mailbox. I'm sure he thought it was early enough in the morning — especially on a Saturday — that no one would see him. But there he was *carrying* his Cocker Spaniel to the mailbox. How embarrassing!

Most cattlemen have an image to uphold when it comes to their dogs. A ranch dog is as valuable to the owner as an extra hired hand. The dog can usually replace a human or two when it comes to rounding up cattle, separating one from the herd, or even guarding the owner from an overprotective momma cow while he tags or medicates a newborn calf. But a Cocker Spaniel — I don't think so.

The breed of a dog is as important to the status of a rancher as the model of pickup he drives. Just as a Ford, Chevy or Dodge (no imports, please) means success, the breed of dog for a cattleman has to be a Border Collie, Australian Shepherd, Blue-heeler, Red-heeler, Wire-mouthed-heeler, or maybe even a Catahoula. But *not* a Cocker Spaniel.

Now, if you think I'm overexaggerating a little, it's only because I speak from experience. Four years ago, after ten years of forbidding my wife to have a house dog (tip for newlyweds: never *forbid* your wife anything), she and the kids walked in with a half Chihuahua, half Miniature Dachshund that soon became part of the family.

A few weeks ago, I needed to run to the local feed store to pick up some mineral for the cows. The dog jumped in the truck, and I was in too much of a hurry to get her out. As I pulled into the parking lot at the feed store, I parked between two farm trucks. One truck had a Blue-heeler in the back and the other had a Border Collie. They looked at the yapping little lap dog as if it could be their next mouth-sized meal. I knew the danger of embarrassment existed, but thought I could run in, get my mineral and get out before any of the locals could see this little excuse for a dog. Wrong.

Before I could get the check written, a neighbor walked in. "That's your white truck outside, isn't it?" he asked.

"Yes," I replied rather sheepishly. "Why?"

"Well, you better start keeping your windows rolled up, 'cause a big rat has done gone and jumped in the cab of your truck," he quipped. Everybody started to laugh as they made their way to the door to see for themselves.

I guess I'll have to start going to another feed store from now on, for the shame is just too great. But at least I wasn't *carrying* the dog.

Chicken

"IT TASTES A LITTLE LIKE CHICKEN, don't you think?" asked a friend of mine as we sampled a dish of alligator tail at one of Branson's fancy, shmancy restaurants.

"Only if your chicken had been hit by a truck and laid out on the road for twelve hours before you fixed it," I replied.

I've never understood why people who are trying a new taste sensation seem so obligated to compare it to chicken. But I have heard the comparison over and over again, concerning everything from rattlesnake to shark meat.

The first time I can ever remember hearing the phrase, as a child, was when our neighbors up the creek, Earnest and Lavelle McGinnis, invited my family to supper one evening. Earnest had killed several ground hogs that had been invading his garden, and Lavelle had devised a way of cooking them that she thought was quite appetizing. I couldn't have been more than eight or nine at the time, but I remember so well putting that piece of dark meat in my mouth and fighting the gag reflex harder than I had ever fought it.

"Tastes a little like chicken, don't you think?" Lavelle asked.

"Yes, Ma'am," I said. Surely God wouldn't punish me for lying just this once. Fact of the matter was, it tasted a lot like ground hog. So, from that point on, I swore I would never be guilty of degrading a poor chicken just to have something to say.

Many years later, while spending a month teaching in the People's Republic of China, I had the occasion to sample many new foods. One particular evening, at a banquet hosted by some high-up Chinese government officials, I was experiencing a dish that seemed more unique than usual — even in China. "What is this interesting taste?" I asked the friendly host seated next to me, as I chewed on something with the texture of pencil erasers.

"Chiug Cho" (or at least something similar-sounding in Chinese), answered my host.

"And what might that be in English?" I asked.

"I believe you call them ... slugs," replied the kind man.

"Hummm," I stalled, "tastes a little like chicken."

Cats

LIFE IS SIMPLE, as I've tried to prove many times over. On the other hand, it is not always fair. Case in point ...

I raise beef cattle. I do it, first of all, because I enjoy it and have always done it. I also raise cattle so that my sons can learn responsibility and, at the same time, have some fun while showing them at local fairs. It requires a lot of hard work, and there's certainly not much monetary incentive in most years.

We also raise cats. That is not part of our game-plan as farmers, but our success has been outstanding.

Every winter my sons and I scour the countryside to find the best purebred heifers we can afford. We go to many farms and sales in order to find them, and rack up too many miles on the truck. The original mother cat simply showed up at our farm one day — free, fertile, and ready to reproduce.

Many times show cattle are difficult to breed. I'm sure the difficulty is brought on by the fact that they are usually overfed, pampered, and housed in a totally artificial environment most of their lives. The cats always breed at the very first opportunity as evidenced by almost continuous pregnancy.

The cattle are monitored very closely when calving time is near. We do this because the show cattle will invariably have difficulty calving. The fear is always very real that the calf may be born dead. I always hope the cat will miscarry to keep the population down, but they *never do!*

When we do get newborn calves on the ground in the spring, I'm scared to drive through the pasture to check on them for fear of running over one hidden in the tall foliage. I must admit I've tried to run over the cats, but it's impossible. Those dead ones I see on the road must be the retarded ones.

When one of the calves gets sick, we just as well start digging the hole, for my luck is not good in saving them. When a cat gets sick, we do nothing, but it always lives and gets pregnant before the next change of the moon.

If I could only figure out how to market cat meat, I would surely be a wealthy man. In the meantime, I'll be content with a few cattle, no mice, and a large herd of barn cats. If anyone needs one, call me. You won't be able to beat my price ... anywhere.

Work

MY GOOD FRIEND, Randy, works for a large, multi-national company that manufactures and sells products for the animal health industry. Like many of us, Randy grew up in an Ozarks family with a strong work ethic, but lacking of many of the luxuries that we now take for granted. In other words, he was "dirt poor." Because Randy was lucky enough to be raised in such an economic environment, he realized early in life that to achieve financial success, he would have to work hard, and his hard-working farm background has indeed paid him great dividends over the years.

Randy now heads the entire national sales division for this company and is therefore responsible for hiring, training, and (if need be) firing those sales representatives who fail to be successful. When the CEO of the company recently reviewed a few years' data on the sales force, he was shocked to discover that every single person that Randy had hired was in the top ten in sales, had the lowest level of sick time, and they were all still with the company. He called Randy in for a conference.

"What's your management secret?" the CEO asked, bluntly. "I need to know so the rest of the corporation can benefit from your skill."

"No secret," Randy replied, nonchalantly, "I guess I've just been lucky."

When Randy relayed this story to me a couple of years ago, he laughed at how the CEO thought it was Randy's management skills that somehow had created these people. "I just hire good people," Randy said.

He told me that sooner or later the CEO would discover that his entire sales force speaks with the same accent — and comes from the same knowledge base. Randy is convinced that the only two places left in the United States that raises kids with a strong work ethic are the Midwest and the South. He is also just as convinced that to sell animal health products — you need to have raised farm animals and have a first-hand understanding of the work that is involved. The latter is becoming more and more difficult to find, since many young people today were raised on successful farms but didn't take an active role in the actual "work." However, Randy has devised quite a clever, investigative method for sorting them out.

It seems that almost all graduates have been heavily "coached" on the standard interview techniques. Most will also give the proper answers to the technical questions on economics and marketing. They will all be dressed appropriately, sporting a flawless resume, and will display the acceptable human relations skills needed by large corporations. But, when Randy ends the interview with each prospective employee, he pulls a trick that would make even Columbo proud.

"Just one more question," he will say, when they both rise to end the interview. "When a cow gets up from a laying position, does she get up on her front feet or rear feet first?"

The kids who haven't worked with livestock are stunned and silent, not knowing the answer. The kids who have had to break a sweat, although amused by the question, will quickly reply with the correct answer.

All that money spent on a college education ... and their future depends on an answer not found in a textbook. Randy's hiring record remains intact, and the CEO still doesn't know his secret.

Fertilizer

I TRY TO WASH MY FARM TRUCK at least twice per year — whether it needs it or not. I like to take it to one of those carwashes where friendly and personable young people do all the work for me, and I always select the cheapest and most basic of their 103 different packages. The way I see it, I just want the basic wash to remove six months of mud, dirt, old feed and cow manure.

When I pulled into the carwash last week, there were three energetic young men working the entrance. As they spotted my truck coming toward them, and before I came to a complete stop, one of the young men hurried toward their break room. Another *ran* to the car parking beside me even though it had actually pulled in after I had. The third young man (obviously, the least experienced of the three) walked slowly toward my truck, staring in bewilderment at its filthy condition.

"It looks like you're overdue for a wash," he commented. "Do you want our best wash package?"

"Nope," I replied, "just give me the cheapest plan and ... get it clean."

At the first station, both young people fought the high-powered vacuum for ten minutes as they removed enough dirt and manure from the floorboard to grow a decent wheat crop. From the back of the truck, they tried to gather everything that looked like trash — from empty feed sacks to pop cans. The line behind my truck grew.

At the next station, a water-soaked young man tried to remove the heaviest of the grime with a high-pressure hose. He looked at me and mouthed, "This is a test. Right." I just smiled.

After the truck had gone through the next hundred feet of

water, soap, brushes and blowers, it emerged looking like a different vehicle than the one I drove in. Unfortunately, there was still a good amount of a brownish-green substance directly behind each tire. A cute and perky young lady worked diligently to dry all the excess water from the truck. I walked over and politely asked her if she could scrub off that "stuff" behind the tires.

"Certainly," she responded, "I'll be happy to." After scrubbing for minutes, with no success, she looked at me and asked, "What is this *stuff?*"

It's just cow manure," I replied.

The young lady gagged, grabbed a clean towel and put it over her mouth and rushed away. I picked up her detergent and scrubber and completed the job myself.

I should have told her it was "just fertilizer."

Smells

OVER THE PAST THREE WEEKS, I've had the opportunity to watch entirely too much TV. As much as I love college basketball — I'm tired of it; daytime TV offers nothing of interest to me, and one sitcom begins to resemble every other one after a few nights. About the only interesting thing I've seen lately was a story on one of the many newsmagazine programs that dealt with "smells."

The segment centered on a funny-talking Frenchman, with a multitude of college degrees in everything from science to psychology, that has classified thousands of different aromas, studying their effects on people's moods, appetites and sex drives. I was very disappointed that my favorite fragrances didn't make his program even though I'm certain that I could find thousands of people who would agree with me.

Just a few of the most wonderful "smells" in the world are:

1. Freshly plowed soil — anyone who has ever stood in the middle of forty acres of newly plowed ground can never forget the aroma that's presented to your senses.

2. Recently mowed alfalfa — About three or four hours after cutting, on a warm summer day, there is absolutely nothing that has a more pleasing fragrance.

3. The scent of an afternoon rain on a hot July day — In the Ozarks, we're usually in the middle of a minor or major drought, so this smell may be as much relief as it is aroma, but it pleases the senses, no less.

4. A new pair of leather boots — Since there aren't any harness shops left, this smell of new leather provides many of us with the only chance to experience the aura of cowhide.

Of course, a month later, these same boots can give us one of the most unpleasant fragrances that can exist.

5. Cow manure — This aroma probably comes as a surprise to many of you, but it's true. Unfortunately, the appeal of this scent is dependent entirely upon cattle prices. When feeder cattle are a dollar per pound and fat cattle are in the mid-seventies, there is no sweeter perfume, on the other hand, when feeder cattle fall into the $60 level, it's just the stink of rotting cowpie.

I can't understand how the little Frenchman missed these smells, along with sassafras, diesel fuel, fresh sawdust and baby pig's breath. I guess he was just too busy getting all those degrees to experience the best "smells" in life.

Chicken Squat?

RALPH AND GLADYS HAD LIVED and worked their entire life in the city. When they retired, they fulfilled a lifelong dream by buying a small, run-down, 40-acre farm and proceeded to transform the little farm into a showplace. The elderly couple stocked the farm with every type of domestic livestock they could purchase, including cattle, horses, mules, sheep, goats, geese, turkeys and chickens — especially chickens.

As the local high school agriculture teacher in that little Ozarks community at that time, I had the pleasure of visiting with Ralph and Gladys on an all-too-frequent basis. Both were extremely inquisitive about every minute detail of agricultural science, so I was often the first person they called when they had a question. I could usually answer most of their questions based on personal experience, common sense, logic, or (if all else failed) what I had learned in college. But occasionally Ralph or Gladys would exceed my resources.

One spring afternoon, at the end of the school day, I saw Ralph walking up the sidewalk toward the agriculture building, carrying something in his hand. As he entered my classroom, Ralph was his usual friendly and jovial self, but he had a question. He uncovered a small glass dish covered with plastic wrap. Laying on the dish was a chicken dropping.

"Whatcha' got there, Ralph?" I asked.

"Chicken manure," Ralph answered emphatically, "but what I need to know is — what is the white-colored part in the very center of each chicken dropping?"

I had always had a great dislike for chickens unless they had been rolled in flour and fried. My dislike for the critters had led me to choose the other elective college courses in the section where *Poultry Production* was offered. I didn't know (nor want to know) the answer to Ralph's question. After apologizing for my ignorance, I suggested he contact the Extension

Office where more highly trained personnel might be able to give him an adequate answer. Off he went to the local branch of University Extension. Thirty minutes later, my phone rang.

I immediately recognized Ralph's voice stating, "They didn't know either."

I looked up the address for a bio-chemical laboratory that I had used in the past and gave it to Ralph, suggesting he send the sample to them for analysis.

A couple of weeks later, I ran into Ralph at the local feed store. "Did you find out what that white part in the center of the chicken dropping was?" I asked.

"Yeah," Ralph answered, rather disgruntled.

"Well, don't keep me in suspense," I continued, "what was it?"

Ralph pulled the lab report out of his pocket and showed it to me. At the bottom of the analysis was the final conclusion: *After careful analysis of the enclosed sample, this laboratory concludes that the entire sample, including the "white" part in the middle, is chicken manure.*

I guess if it looks like chicken manure, smells like chicken manure and feels like chicken manure — it probably is chicken manure. If only I'd have taken that poultry course, I could have saved Ralph the ten-dollar lab fee.

Smokin'

I READ A NEWS ARTICLE THE OTHER DAY that dealt with the growing problem of drug abuse in China. The "experts" concluded that the problem was due to the modernization of China through increased industrialization, which had brought about a higher standard of living for its citizens, leaving them with more money in their pockets to spend on the "evils" of the world. I, however, can't help but feel that it is partially my fault.

In 1985, I spent a month in China, along with a group of about 20 other agriculture teachers and professors. The group, in between offering guest lectures at many of China's agricultural universities, got the opportunity to tour several Chinese farms to better understand the problems their country faced in feeding over a billion people. These farms ranged in size from tiny one-acre family farms to large, communist-controlled, communal farms of 2000-3000 acres.

The small plots primarily produced vegetables, flowers and rice. The large farms, which employed thousands of people providing unlimited amounts of hand labor, generally produced cotton, wheat, poultry, dairy, pork, and a crop that I had never seen grown on a large-scale, commercial basis here in the United States — hemp.

We were traveling down a dirt road along the border of one of the large farms the first time I witnessed hemp growth in China. The edge of the field was formed by single wooden poles, suspended by wooden posts for as far as the eye could see. Hemp plants were draped across these poles to dry in the Chinese sun. Since I wasn't sure what they were, I asked (through the interpreter) what was going on there. The farm manager, again through the interpreter, carefully and meticulously explained how the hemp was grown, harvested, cured and processed into the bulk of China's packing products, such as boxes, baskets, twine, rope and even some crude paper products. I was both surprised and amazed.

"Do you have any problems with your workers using the plant for its intoxicating effect on the body?" I asked.

The farm manager seemed confused as I asked more questions about the hemp farm. Realizing that I must need to give a little background information, I had the interpreter explain to the manager how hemp is illegal in the United States because it is an illicit drug that, when smoked, can alter the mind much like alcohol.

The farm manager looked at me strangely and asked, "You mean you can smoke this plant?"

Sorry, China.

Space, the Final Frontier

REPRESENTATIVES FROM 150 NATIONS will gather in Japan this week to discuss the issues associated with "global warming." The U.S. delegation should (but won't) include two farmers from Southwest Missouri and my seventh-grade son. I believe that Wayne, Jimmie and Seth could provide pertinent information regarding some of the myths concerning this phenomenon.

Wayne and Jimmie raise hundreds of tons of high quality hay each year for area livestock producers. The quantity of hay they produce requires them to be in the field almost every week throughout the summer — including the 4th of July. This past 4th of July found Wayne cutting hay early that morning while Jimmie brought his children to the Greene County 4-H fair. After Jimmie got the kids and cattle settled at the fair, he returned home to take over the hay-cutting duties from Wayne. When he arrived at the field, Jimmie was shocked to see his father wearing a heavy coat.

As Wayne stopped the tractor and mower, Jimmie asked, "What's the deal wearing a coat on the 4th of July?"

"I think you'll need me to leave it with you. It's cold out here," Wayne replied.

"No thanks," Jimmie responded, "passersby might think I'm crazy." After only two rounds, Jimmie had to stop and go to the house to get that coat.

The need for a coat on the 4th of July in Southwest Missouri should be ample proof that global warming hasn't happened yet — but if more evidence is needed, my son Seth could help out.

I was helping him with a school science experiment earlier this fall when, to prove a point, the textbook instructed him to fill a glass three-fourths full of water, then add ice cubes until the water level was even with the top of the glass. This caused some of the ice cubes to float above the top of the glass. In a few hours after all the ice had melted, the water level was below the top of the glass. "How can that be?" Seth asked.

Eager to impress my son with my vast knowledge (not to mention that I had already read the next two pages in his science book), I informed him that ice is one of the few substances that actually expands when it freezes, therefore taking up more space than the water it once was.

"So if the polar icebergs, 90% of which are below the water's surface, melt due to global warming, the oceans would actually shrink in volume instead of flooding islands and low areas?" he asked.

"Uh, yeah, I guess," I confidently answered.

Too bad these three individuals won't be at the conference this week.

I Got Gas

I BOUGHT A PICK-UP TRUCK just last Christmas; it died this past weekend. I don't mean it shut off while running; I mean it DIED. With a list price that was half of what I gave for my farm 12 years ago, I didn't hesitate in calling the toll-free assistance number to have it towed to the dealership where it was purchased. The service manager was nice enough, but quickly informed me that noon was closing time on Saturdays, and Monday would be the soonest they could get to my truck.

Knowing that a loaner truck was part of the super-duper warranty, I politely asked the manager which truck I would be driving home. "I'm sorry," he apologized, "but all of our loaner trucks are checked out."

"I know I could use some exercise," I replied, "but walking 20 miles is a bit more than I'm used to."

"Oh, we'll get you something to drive," the manager said with a nod and a wink; then he walked behind a partition to use the phone.

A few minutes later he reappeared. "You're in luck," he said. "We just got a good used trade-in you can take home for the weekend. Come on; let me show you."

As we walked outside together, we were greeted by the biggest, longest, blackest Cadillac I have ever seen. "Drive it like it was yours," was all he said.

Having driven a pick-up for the past 15 years, it was awkward enough just being in a car, much less a huge, tank-like Cadillac. As I sat in the driver's seat, I was surrounded by more gadgets and electronics than you would find in the cockpit of a 747 jetliner. When I turned the key on, the seat moved, bells sounded, and I was scared. As I left the dealership, the electronic reading on the fuel gauge informed me that I had two gallons of fuel, so I stopped and put in some gas.

Pulling out onto the highway from the gas station, I realized

I needed ten more acres to turn this monster around. As the rear wheel bounded up over the curb, the front bumper missed an oncoming car by a fraction of an inch, and that poor driver was handicapped. I know, because he spoke sign language.

I must admit that once out on the highway and up to cruising speed, the Caddy drove like the aforementioned 747, because just three miles from home I had to stop for gas again.

Once home, I realized I needed a couple of small bales of hay for my sons' show calves. The hay is 15 miles away, over at my father's farm. However, the guy did tell me to drive it like it was my own. I put in more gas.

At my dad's place, the two bales of hay fit nicely in the trunk of the Cadillac with the trunk lid roped down so as not to flop in the wind. The Cadillac looked so nice with hay bales sticking out the rear, I decided to put a couple of steel fence posts in the back seat and sticking out the rear window just for effect.

On the way home, I stopped once more for gas. While putting fuel in for the fourth time that day, a Lincoln Continental with Texas plates pulled up on the other side of the pump. A stately gentleman in a cowboy hat got out and stared curiously at the hay and the posts in "my" Cadillac.

"You a rancher, too?" drawled the Texan.

"Yep," I answered.

"How big's your spread?" he asked, reaching for the nozzle.

"I don't really know for sure," I replied, "but I can't drive around it on less than half a tank of gas."

The Texan was impressed.

Burger Substitute

JUST HOW CHEAP are cattle prices right now? Let me explain ...

Fast food restaurants have always been accused of using "filler" substances in their beef patties. These "filler" substances have always been some product that was much cheaper than beef. Sometimes these accusations have been substantiated and sometimes not, but the suspicion has always been there.

When I was in college, back in the early seventies, one of my roommates was in the College of Veterinary Medicine. One day my roommate had a lab assignment. For this assignment, he was to go to five different fast food restaurants, purchase a hamburger from each, and run a chemical analysis on all of them to determine the content of each burger. From this research, my roommate found everything from horse meat to soybeans in those "all beef" burgers. (I'm sure my readers might also recall the now infamous burgers containing kangaroo meat a few years ago.)

Since that time, the diet of many Americans has changed. Spurred on by the animal-rights groups, beef has been under attack. Companies wanting to cash in on this paranoia found a new market. Thus, you can now purchase "veggie burgers" at many of these same fast food establishments. These burgers, which are advertised and sold as burger substitute, are made primarily from soybeans which can be textured and colored to look and taste like real meat. I have not sampled these burgers myself because:
1. I raise cattle
2. I don't believe beef is unhealthy

However, I have been told by some that these veggie burgers have a flavor very similar to beef.

All of this leads me to the latest accusation. Given the fact that live cattle are cheaper than they have been in many, many years, and soybeans are nearing a price that is an all-time high, could it be possible that these fast food giants are using beef as the "filler" in veggie burgers? It could happen ... so you *animal-righters* out there ... better watch out for those veggie burgers. It just may be that the oil dripping out of the rare ones didn't come from any soybean.

Five Ways to Excel

I'VE JUST FINISHED REVIEWING a few of the new Show-Me Standards. You may have seen or heard of these over the past few weeks, as they are supposed to represent a set of goals that Missouri wants their high school graduates to obtain before they finish school. Supposedly, these standards were formulated by a committee of teachers, parents, citizens and bureaucrats to make sure Missouri has better schools and better prepared students.

Although I've been a teacher for 21 years, I missed the invitation list to participate in the formulation of these standards. As you might expect, I have a few standards that I think should have been included:

1. Make sure the student can read. But, more importantly, make sure they can understand what they have read. It amazes me every fall, when I get a fresh batch of college freshmen, how very few of them can read a set of instructions for completing an exam and actually do what the instructions tell them.

2. Make sure the student can write. I'm not talking about the qualities needed for the next best-selling book — just good, plain, to-the-point English that the average person can read and understand what the writer is trying to say.

3. Make sure the student can perform basic functions of arithmetic. The majority of my college freshmen can't convert fractions to decimals, decimals to percentages, nor figure interest on money. (Wouldn't you like to sell them a credit card!)

4. What was the student's attendance record in school? This

one is not a standard, simply a way of finding out how dependable the prospective employee might be on his/her new job. As a small business owner, absenteeism and tardiness are the two biggest reasons we have to terminate employees. It doesn't take a rocket scientist to correlate school attendance to work attendance.

5. This last standard shouldn't have to be taught by the schools so, Parents, listen up. Make sure the youngster has some manners and can respect authority. Nothing pleases employers (or college professors) more than the words please; thank you; yes, sir/ma'am.

I realize this list is pretty short and doesn't contain much, if any, educational jargon. I can assure you, however, with some degree of confidence, that a student who excels in all five of the above standards will be successful, regardless of the career they choose.

Shock

AN OLD FRIEND STOPPED BY the other day for an overdue visit. Like me, my friend has been in the beef cattle business all of his life. Unlike me, my friend is solely dependent upon the cattle business to support himself and his family. As one might suspect, low cattle prices, high feed prices, and a shortage of hay from last summer's drought had my friend more than a little depressed.

"I just don't know if I can take it any more," he confessed. "A couple of bad years seem to wipe out all the gains I made when cattle prices were strong."

After talking with him for awhile, it was clear to me that he wasn't in danger of losing the farm or anything nearly that drastic, but he was dejected to the extent that he needed someone to tell him that he *could* take it — and survive.

"Have I ever told you about Zach and the electric fence?" I asked.

"Nope," he replied.

So ... I began.

Every spring, I use an electric fence to fence off 40 acres of my open pasture to cut for hay. This is usually done in April, so I can apply a heavier rate of fertilizer than the pastures get, as well as spare all the plant growth from any grazing by my cow herd. My youngest son, Zach, had never been old enough to be out and around the electric fence until he was about four; therefore I had never taught him the precautions of playing around the fence.

That year, knowing that the ever-inquisitive Zach would be around the fence, I instructed him to NEVER touch the shiny new wire.

"Why?" was the obvious question of a four-year-old.

"Because it will shock you," I replied.

"What's a shock?"

I tried, in my best four-year-old vocabulary, to explain what an electrical shock was and what it felt like. The best analogy I could come up with, so that Zach might understand, was that it felt somewhat like a wasp sting. I had observed him tearing down a wasp nest the previous summer — with wasps covering the nest. I knew he remembered that!

The next morning, I got up early and went into town after supplies. When I returned around mid-morning, I went into the house to find my wife and oldest son around the kitchen table reading the newspaper. "Where's Zach," I asked.

My wife said she hadn't seen him since he went outside to play several minutes ago. I wasn't concerned, but figured I'd find him to see if he wanted to go with me to check cows. When I stepped out onto the deck of our home, I saw Zach down by the electric fence, and he seemed to be holding something. Curiously, I walked closer without Zach noticing me. As I got close enough to see what was going on, I was surprised to see Zach, standing barefoot in the wet grass, holding one of the barn cats in his hands. He would touch the cat's nose to the electric fence, and the cat would scream simultaneously with a jump and wince from Zach himself.

"What on earth are you doing?" I yelled.

"Oh, Dad," Zach acknowledged. "This cat ... he thinks he can't take it, but he can," was the reply, as he added, "I just don't know how much more *I* can take."

My friend conceded that it was a lot like the cattle business today.

Ozonics

ALL OF THE PUBLICITY and attention given to "ebonics" over the last few weeks has made me more than a little jealous. For those of you who might not have heard about it, "ebonics" (a combination of the words ebony and phonics) is the name given to the "language" that many African-Americans speak. The Oakland, California school system has chosen (with many state and federal grants, no doubt) to include this class in their school system to raise the self-esteem of their black students. You see, "ebonics" allows the mispronunciation and spelling of many words, disregards proper sentence structure, and even encourages the use of double negatives because many African-Americans have "cultural and genetic tendencies to talk this way."

The reason I am so jealous is because those of us born and raised in the Ozarks have cultural and genetic tendencies to talk the way we do, and I would hope that our schools could get a few million dollars of state and federal grant money to teach "ozonics" (ozark phonics) in our school system. I'm also upset that my English teacher, Mrs. Madge Parker, didn't try to raise my self-esteem when I spoke or wrote incorrect English instead of swatting my hands with a ruler!

With "ozonics," students would be praised instead of penalized for writing and speaking words like, "I figger the guvment owes us this'n."

Little kids in the Ozarks could also be rewarded for sentences such as, "We got everthang we need in them thar hills."

And, lastly, the double negatives of ebonics can't even compare to the quintuple negatives of the "ozonics" language. Sentences such as, "I ain't got no job, but I don't want none, nohow," would be considered intellectual, if not downright eloquent.

School administrators across the Ozarks need to get busy

writing grant proposals to incorporate "ozonics" into their curriculum. Remember ... thar's hunnerts and hunnerts of dollars fur us'ns that's hurtin'.

Punishment

THE OZARKS ARE REALLY CRACKING DOWN on criminals. I know this to be true because I've read it in the papers and heard it on the radio in two separate stories this past week.

Item #1 — Between 50 and 100 shad minnows were found murdered in a pond somewhere close to Springfield. Never mind that the sole purpose in life, for a shad minnow, is to be eaten by bigger fish, cranes or maybe a snapping turtle. The Conservation Department, with help from the Department of Natural Resources, local law enforcement and quite likely the IRS, ATF and FBI will track down the offender whose septic tank overflowed and brutally ended the life of these minnows, and bring them to justice.

Item #2 — Our neighbors to the south, in Branson, have decided to increase the punishment and step up enforcement for the act of driving nails into the hearts of trees in that town. It seems that some dastardly villains have so little regard for the stately trees in that town that they attach garage sale signs to those trees with nails that sometimes injure or even kill them. The punishment for those criminals caught in the act will be both swift and severe.

Meanwhile, in southern California, my prediction is that O.J. will never serve a day is prison. He had better be thankful he's not on trial in the Ozarks, because I'll bet money that the bloody glove caused the early and untimely death of more than a few fruit flies. Nor would I be surprised if that swinging knife didn't cause some serious injury to a tree or shrub in the yard that night.

In the Ozarks, we might go ahead and hang him for those crimes.

Budgeting

SOME VERY GOOD FRIENDS OF MINE are going through a difficult budget crisis in their household right now.

These two people have been together for a long time and have succeeded in many aspects of life. They have built a successful business, raised a wonderful family and contributed to many worthwhile organizations. But now they have a problem.

Bill (not his real name) likes to think that he runs the family, but Newt (not her real name) really controls the finances by initiating all the payments and spending. Somehow, over the past 23 months, my friends have run up huge deficits by spending much more than they were taking in. These large monthly deficits have resulted in an almost insurmountable debt that hovers over them like a cloud of impending disaster.

Newt has devised a way to balance their budget within the next seven months if they can only reduce the rate at which their spending is increasing. Bill is not sure it can be done so quickly, but thinks that with smaller sacrifices their budget can be balanced in ten months. By extending the pain out over ten months, Bill believes he can keep the big white house they live in and won't have to give up his favorite toy, a bass boat he calls "Bass Force I."

They both took their plans for straightening out their monetary mess to the banker who has financed them for years and years. Thinking that the banker would accept one or the other of their plans, they were shocked when he told them he had no choice but to foreclose on all their assets unless they could balance their budget immediately, as well as begin making significant payments on the debt they had incurred.

"But what about my mother in the expensive nursing home," Bill cried. "And my poor relatives that I'm supporting; and my kids going to college; and all the people who work for my company," he continued.

"I'm sorry, but business is business," replied the banker. "You just can't spend more money than you make."

Good advice that both people and governments should remember.

"V"

I LOVE THIS TIME OF YEAR. There's a chill in the air, the leaves are turning, and overhead the geese are heading south. In my mind, nothing compares to the serenity created by being outside on a cool autumn morning and looking upward in response to the honking geese. There, just a few hundred feet overhead, is the imperfect "V" created by these majestic creatures, flying their intricate formation that constantly changes like flowing water.

I've always marveled at the precision with which these geese fly. My interest in their flying patterns and migration habits led me to a recent lecture presented by an authority on the Canadian goose. The lecture proved extremely interesting as the expert explained how the "V" flying pattern was the most aerodynamic. This allows the geese in the back to take advantage of the drafts created by the leader and makes their flight much easier. The expert went on to explain how the leader keeps changing every few minutes, thus allowing another member of the flock to take on the tough job of breaking through the wind resistance. He concluded his presentation by explaining that the constant honking is only a way for the followers to cheer on the leader at the point of the "V," who really has the toughest job.

I was so impressed with this person's expertise, I stuck around after the conclusion to visit with him individually. After introducing myself and complimenting him on his enlightening presentation, I asked him a question that has always intrigued me. "Why," I asked, "is one side of the 'V' always longer than the other side?"

Expecting some long scientific answer that would ease my curiosity, I was shocked when he looked at me with a smile and answered, "There are more geese in the long side of the 'V'."

Sometimes even I try to make life too complicated.

Illness

PARENTS DON'T TREAT childhood illnesses like they did when I was a kid. Today's children should thank their lucky stars.

When a child gets sick in this day and time, the parent either takes them to a pediatrician for a quick exam and a prescription for the latest antibiotic that works wonders, or goes to the local pharmacy where they can find an entire section of miracle-medicines just for kids. These medicines work on everything from the common cold to ingrown toenails with flavors, colors and gimmicks that make even the most finicky of kids "want" to take them.

During my childhood years, any illness that I ever experienced would bring a diagnosis from one or both my parents to the effect of, "All you need is a little cleaning out." Translated for today's generation, that means they were going to the medicine shelf in the back room to get a bottle of one of the following:

    A. Syrup of Black Draught
    B. Syrup of Pepsin
    C. Syrup of cow manure (since they all tasted the same, anyway)

I never knew whether these medicines were laxatives, elixirs or snake oils, but I did know they all tasted pretty much the same — excruciatingly terrible. I have no idea what they were made from, but the taste would indicate a possible mixture of uncooked molasses and rotting walnut hulls.

The black draught medicine is probably the reason I never liked Porter Waggoner's music. Black draught was the longtime sponsor of Porter's Saturday afternoon TV show, and I just never could appreciate the music knowing that it was sponsored by something that caused me such great discomfort.

As far as the "cleaning out" goes, no one could dispute its effectiveness. These medicines could clean you out faster than a D-8 Cat could clean out a thicket of sassafras saplings. On the other hand, the cure usually made you feel worse than the illness you had to begin with.

So when my seven-year-old whines and complains that a cherry-flavored medicine, with cartoon characters on the dispenser, tastes bad, I don't have much sympathy.

Semen

A COUPLE OF WEEKS AGO I had ordered a few units of bull semen to artificially inseminate some purebred cows and heifers my boys own. I had given explicit instructions to the company shipping the semen, that it positively *had* to arrive by Wednesday, November 29, for we were leaving for a trip out of town on Thursday. I knew the frozen semen would thaw and therefore ruin if delivered while we were away and before we returned on Sunday. The guy at the semen company assured me that it would probably be there on Tuesday before we left.

Tuesday came and went. No semen.

Wednesday came and went. Again, no semen.

Wednesday night I called the semen company, and the guy apologized all over himself for not getting it shipped out until that very day. The apology may have made him feel better, but I was in even more of a panic. I had five units of fairly expensive semen in a UPS truck somewhere between north Missouri and my farm.

My wife was going to meet me at the airport at 2:30 on Thursday, so that we could fly out together to a meeting in Nevada. Just in case it might arrive before my wife left home, I had given her exact directions for transferring the semen from the shipping tank into the permanent tank we have at home.

At about 1:30, as my wife was hurriedly completing her last-minute packing, the doorbell rang. Judy looked out the window and saw the familiar UPS truck in the driveway. She ran down the stairs, slung the door open and very excitedly said, "Thank goodness, you've brought the semen I need!"

Shocked and a bit nervous, the delivery man said, "No, ma'am, I just have a package for you."

Evidently, the man had no idea what was in the container

he was delivering, nor was he quite sure what my wife had meant, but Judy described it as the quickest and quietest she had ever signed for a package in her life.

Teeth

THOSE OF US WHO ARE INVOLVED with agriculture on an everyday basis are sometimes a little reluctant to accept "non-aggies" into our circle. That reluctance is even magnified when an outsider moves in with the attitude that they can surely succeed, even where we have failed, because they know more than we do.

When I was a young boy growing up in the Ozarks, I remember such an individual buying a farm up the creek from ours. The gentleman was from a large northeastern city. He was well educated, had been a success in a non-agriculture business, and thought he could move to the hills where inexpensive land would allow him to make a quick fortune raising baby calves that he could buy cheaply from the many dairy farmers in the area.

My father would usually buy and raise about 50 of those bottle calves each year himself. Dad had developed quite a talent for keeping them alive and actually made a little money on them most years. But then, this new neighbor was going to "show" the rest of us how to really be successful raising these bottle babies, with plans to raise 2000 head per year.

The neighbor would really irritate Dad whenever they would cross paths at the local general store by telling my father, "You had better get big or get out."

"We'll see how big he gets," I remember my father saying as we were leaving in the old truck.

It couldn't have been more than a couple of months before we began to suspect there was trouble at the newcomer's farm. Those hundreds of buzzards circling in the sky over the farm to the south of ours was proof enough. And that stench of a smell wasn't coming from our outhouse. That neighbor had problems.

I suppose it was hard for our neighbor to swallow enough

of his pride to come and ask Dad for advice, but that is just what he did. Dad consented to go over and see if he could figure out the problem, and I couldn't wait to tag along.

At ten or eleven years old, even I knew what the problem was as soon as we set foot on the farm. Scours are hard enough to control when you're raising just a few baby calves, but a couple of hundred calves together made the problem next to impossible to control in those days.

I was extremely puzzled, however, at my dad's actions after we arrived. Instead of simply telling the neighbor what the problem was and suggesting a remedy, Dad was going up to several of the calves and looking in their mouths.

"Where did you get these calves?" Dad asked.

"I've been picking them up at different farms around here," the neighbor replied. "Why do you ask?"

Not responding to the neighbor's question, Dad asked, "How much have they been costing you?"

"Most of them cost about $20 each," the neighbor replied with a confused look on his face.

"Well, I don't know how to tell you this," my father explained, "but they've been selling you deformed calves."

"Deformed?" cried the neighbor.

"Yep," answered Dad, "there's not a one of them that have any upper teeth."

"What will I do?" asked the neighbor.

"I hate to see a man taken advantage of," said Dad, "so I'll give you $5 a head for the ones you have left, if you want to sell them."

As we left with a truckload of cheap, but sick, calves, Dad reminded me of what I should have learned that day. First, there's no such thing as a quick and easy fortune. Secondly, never get big in something you know nothing about, and thirdly — always buy low.

Fathering

THEY WERE SITTING on the front row at the livestock auction as I took a seat in the row behind and to the right of them. A man in his early to mid-thirties, dressed in working-man's clothing and wearing a hat that showed years of use and care, was seated by his five-year-old son. The boy was dressed just like his dad, except his black cowboy hat was cleaner and his boots were absent the manure that was on his father's.

As the auction began, three Holstein baby calves were in the ring waiting on the auctioneer to start the sale. The man with the little boy bought them, paying the going price (which isn't much) for the calves. A couple of beef-cross calves came in next, and the man bought these as well, but paid quite a bit more for them. Then a baby beef calf was driven into the sale ring. This mouse-colored calf was, without a doubt, the best quality baby calf to be sold this evening. The calf had tremendous bone and thickness and appeared to be very healthy, probably the survivor of a difficult birth that had claimed its mother. It was also the "cutest" little baby calf at the auction.

"That's the one I really want," I overheard the little boy tell his dad as he tugged on the sleeve of his father's coat.

The man began bidding very aggressively on this cute little calf. A cattle trader, sitting in the back of the crowd, started to run the price up on him. Evidently, the trader had noticed how the man had bought all the previous baby calves, regardless of price, and figured his competition would simply make the calf bring more.

I winced a little as the trader quit bidding, leaving the man owning a good calf, but with a lot more money invested than the calf was really worth.

It was a very short sale that night, wrapping up in about 30 minutes. As everyone got up to leave, I heard an older gentleman say to the man who bought the calves, "They kinda got to you on that last calf, didn't they?"

"If I was in the business of raising cattle," he replied, "then I guess you could say I paid too much. But, you see, I'm in the business of raising kids."

A simple man, that the world needs more of.

Coffee

It's funny how some traditions and customs change over the years and others seem to live on forever.

I spent this past weekend helping my parents sort through 60 years of belongings to sell, in order for them to have room as they moved to a smaller home. In the bottom of some old boxes, I found a set of deep-dish saucers with a like set of china coffee cups. As a child, I had watched my father drink his breakfast coffee every morning, by pouring the steaming hot liquid from the cup into the saucer and gently blowing over the top of the coffee to cool it before sipping it from the saucer itself. It reminded me that I had also observed my grandparents and many others from that generation perform this coffee ritual. I haven't seen anyone drink coffee from a saucer in 30 years and I wondered why.

As I pondered this phenomenon, I couldn't help but realize that this was a very practical method to cool the coffee. In fact, if we still practiced this ritual, there would not have been a multi-million-dollar lawsuit a couple of years ago against a fast food chain because a customer was burned by coffee that was "too hot." Of course, most restaurants don't even give you a saucer with your coffee cup any more — and if they do, the saucer certainly isn't made to pour the coffee into, unless you only need a couple of teaspoonfuls at a time.

I suppose our rush-hurry-always-late lifestyles won't even begin to allow us the time to drink coffee at the kitchen table in the morning. And I really can't see the fast food giants giving us a styrofoam saucer at the drive-thru window either.

I miss those times when everything happened at a little slower pace and we all had time to stop and smell the coffee ... from a saucer.

Butter

AS PART OF MY JOB, I spend a good deal of time every spring helping to set up and conduct contests for FFA members across the state. One of these contests involves the tasting and testing of dairy foods, with a section of the contest devoted to distinguishing the difference between real and imitation dairy products. This year, I decided to have a little fun of my own, just to see how much the students knew beyond the limits of the contest.

"Where does butter come from?" I asked one of the contestants after a recent contest.

"Well, butter comes from milk, of course," answered the student wearing the blue jacket.

Expecting that obvious answer, I continued, "But do you know how butter is made from milk?"

"They make it at the butter factory," came the final reply.

The first time I ever heard of a "butter factory," I envisioned hundreds of men and women sitting in a line, all shaking half-gallon jars of cream, for this is the method that was used in the Crownover home when I was a kid.

We milked an old Jersey cow ... by hand ... twice daily. As the cream rose to the top of this whole milk, Mom would skim it off and store the cream until she had about a quart of fat-rich cream to put into a half-gallon mason jar. She would then wait until that time when she thought I had absolutely nothing left to do, and then she would make me shake that jar of cream until it turned into butter. I suppose it took no longer than five to ten minutes of violent shaking, but it surely seemed like an hour back then.

Some of our wealthier neighbors had a butter churn with a hand crank attached to a wooden paddle wheel that set in a gallon container, but not us. The mason jar with a twelve-year-old boy attached was the method of choice to obtain delicious yellow butter from plain white milk.

Now, I could have gone into a 30-minute lecture to this young FFA member on how butter is obtained from milk, but in this modern era of agriculture, I simply nodded and smiled, and said, "Yes, butter is made from milk at the butter factory."

Lifestyle

SINCE MY FARM IS SURROUNDED by three other beef farms, all with bulls in their pastures, I have always had trouble with bulls. When I bring a bull over from the other farm for breeding season, he always finds it necessary to establish his dominance (or lack of) in the first few weeks. I spend most every morning of late May and June repairing fences that were torn up the night before by fighting bulls. That bulls have to know who is the toughest is a simple fact of nature. However, this spring started out a little different.

In March I went to Sedalia and bought an outstanding quality bull at the state sale for one of the major beef breeds. The bull was halter broke, exceedingly gentle and easy-handling. I kept him at my dad's farm until it was time to bring him over to my place for the breeding season. The first week at my farm was unbelievable since I had absolutely no fences to fix. I was busy making hay and elated that this bull was so different from past bulls. He wasn't fighting any of the neighbors' bulls.

After that first week, when I finally got some time away from haying, I started watching the bull more closely. Not only did this bull not show the aggression toward the neighbors' bulls, he didn't show the "affection" toward my cows that were in need of his "affection." Day after day of observing different cows in heat, my prize bull seemed more interested in playing with the Holstein steers that shared the pasture. Not knowing whether this was a physical problem or simply a lifestyle choice, I called the farm where he was purchased. The gentleman kindly offered me a replacement bull. I had no alternative but to accept the replacement.

I can only assume that the bull I returned is now 1800 pounds of hamburger, since there is not much of a demand for bulls that won't breed. The new bull seems to be very happy with my lonely cows. As for me, I'm back to fixing fence every morning.

Nature

IN THE NEWS RECENTLY was a report of the death of an animal rights activist in Spain. It seems that a young lady was video-taping the ceremonial running of the bulls to illustrate, to the general public, how cruel and inhumane this tradition is. Unfortunately, the bull didn't know she was trying to help him, and gored her to death.

As a farmer, I have little use for anyone who intentionally abuses livestock. Animals are what make us a living, and it would be stupid to do anything to them that makes them suffer and therefore produce less of the milk, meat, wool, eggs or whatever they provide for us. At the same time, I have just as little use for these misguided, holier-than-thou people who, for some odd reason, place animals on a higher plane than people.

What this poor young lady should have realized is that any bull, whether it is a Spanish fighting bull or one you have raised on the bottle from the time it was born, can turn on you at some time and try to make hamburger out of you instead of the other way around. Bulls always fight each other and many times — people. That is the natural order as far as a bull is concerned.

This story caused me to remember my first encounter with the animal rights people. It was 1975, and I was teaching agriculture at Alton High School, over in Oregon County. There was a group of people in that community who got together once every month to fight their roosters. An animal rights group from the St. Louis area had gotten word of this and persuaded a reluctant rural police department to raid the next cock-fight. On the day of the raid, the animal rights group followed up the law enforcement people in a shiny new truck with about 20 stainless steel cages to put the birds in and take them to their "safety." After the raid and the tickets were issued, the animal rights group loaded about 40-50 fighting roosters in the 20 cages for transport back to St. Louis. If you will follow the simple math, you will see that there were at least two roosters in every cage.

Once again, the animal rights group learned a very difficult lesson. Roosters fight each other in a natural setting. The roosters didn't know the people were trying to help them. They simply killed each other inside the cages.

Water

I AM IN "HOT WATER" WITH MY WIFE. Or maybe a better description would be "no water."

Sometime last week, lightning evidently struck our well pump, but it didn't quit pumping until late Saturday night. Sunday morning found me calling every pump repairman within 20 miles while my wife went over to a neighbor's house to shower. The boys and I decided to stay home and stink.

A very nice young man was kind enough to come over on Sunday morning to check out our situation. I was still hoping that it was something simple that could be fixed with a screwdriver and pair of pliers. "Nope," he stated, "I'm afraid your pump will have to be replaced. How soon do you need it?"

My reply was simply, "Well, I am married."

He understood what I was saying, but he explained how he had made plans with his family for Sunday afternoon and he probably couldn't get in touch with his helper anyway. I tried to be understanding as well, and agreed that early Monday morning would be acceptable.

The pump repairman left, and I went inside to break the news to my wife, Judy, who owns a small business herself and frequently has to work weekends even when family plans are already made, was not nearly as understanding as I had been. She left immediately to go to the grocery story to purchase meals that could be prepared without water (I forgot to mention that we were having guests over for dinner Sunday evening). When she returned, her first words were, "And just how are our guests supposed to use the bathroom?"

Having grown up without the benefit of running water, I was ready for that question. "The man can join me down at the barn, and I'll bring up a milk can of water from the pond to keep one toilet operating for you ladies," I replied. Judy was not amused.

For those of you familiar with the expression — Hell hath no fury like that of a woman scorned — you need to meet my wife after two days without running water. A scorned woman would have been a welcome sight around the Crownover house.

Words

NOT ONLY DO PEOPLE from different parts of this wonderful country talk differently, they use different words to describe the same things. This can, many times, lead to grave misunderstandings.

My roommates in college were all from North Missouri. The first time we all went to the grocery store to stock up on food, they were greatly amused when I referred to the grocery bag as a "paper poke." They were even more amused when I asked, "Just what do you'ns use to put your 'vittles' in?"

When I lived in Mississippi, I had to learn an entirely new language. One Monday morning one of the professors I worked with told me he had "carried" his wife to eat at a new restaurant the previous weekend. Having met his rather robust wife before, I asked him if he had hurt his back. He was not amused and quickly taught me that in the Deep South, *carry* means *take*.

But the best story of my inability to communicate with non-Ozarkians occurred this past summer. While in Texas to attend a livestock show, a friend and I decided to drive out to a little ranch west of Abilene to look at some prospective show heifers. We only knew the general location of the ranch. As we got close to where I thought the ranch was, I saw an old cowboy working on a windmill at the side of the dirt road we were traveling. I stopped and asked him if he knew where the ranch in question was. He did, and proceeded to give me directions. "Y'all need to keep goin' west on this road for 'bout another mile and a half," he instructed. "You'll see a tank on the south side of the road and then y'all need to turn south on the very next farm-to-market road, and it'll take you directly by the ranch."

I thanked him, and we took off. Easy enough directions to follow, except that after traveling at least five more miles, I hadn't seen any tank anywhere amongst the mesquite brush. I retraced my path to the cowboy at the windmill. "Sir," I asked, "was that tank you were talking about an oil tank or a water tank?"

The weathered old man looked at me and asked, "Where y'all from?"

"Missouri," I replied.

"I forgot," he said. "Y'all call 'em ponds instead of tanks up north."

"You call a *pond,* a *tank?*" I asked.

"Yep, that's what they're called in Texas."

"Well, that's the craziest thing I've ever heard."

"It may be crazy to you, but I'm not the one that's lost, am I?"

Economics

BLACK WALNUTS ARE BRINGING $10 per hundred this year. Oh ... to be a kid again.

As a youngster, I picked up more than a few tons of walnuts over the years, sold them for only two to three dollars per hundred, and developed a serious love-hate relationship with the nut. I hated to pick them up because it was hard work for a small kid to crawl around on their hands and knees all day long. My hands would become permanently stained to the point that only a new layer of skin would rid me of the color. The only thing remotely fun was climbing the trees to knock down the remaining nuts clinging to the branches, and even then, I would get thumped in the head by those directly above me. But ...

I loved the money. Picking up walnuts was about the only thing a young kid could do back then and get immediate gratification in the form of cash. So I would just keep telling myself how rich I was going to be after a trip to the huller — 1200 pounds of walnuts would become 400 pounds of hulled nuts, which would become $10 to a 10-year-old boy. I was rich.

Wealth is always relative, isn't it? Walnuts are worth four times what they were when I was a boy. The minimum wage is about four times what it was in my youth. Gasoline costs about four times what it did in 1962. Teachers make about four times as much as they did back then, and cars cost a little more than four times as much as comparable models of the early sixties. I guess I'm still rich.

While the rest of society believes that the economy is dependent upon the prime interest rate, consumer price index and the New York Stock Exchange, we here in the Ozarks are smart enough to realize that it's really the price paid for black walnuts that is the leading economic indicator.

Welfare

MY FIRST REAL-LIFE ENCOUNTER with the American system of Welfare was not a good one. That may be the reason I remain so skeptical of the system today.

Growing up in rural Ozark County, Missouri, we would most certainly have been labeled as "poor." But since everyone else I knew was also poor, it didn't really matter. There wasn't much of a social ladder in and around Gainesville, and if there had been, I'll bet we could of spit over it from a sitting position. Anyway, as a 12- or 13-year-old boy, my needs were pretty practical. I had my eye on a new Timex watch at the local Western Auto store. My father had said that maybe sometime this year we could afford to pay the $7.95 that it cost.

Early one spring, it looked as if we were going to have quite a lot of extra hay left over from a relatively mild winter, so we let the word out that we had hay for sale. A neighbor from a few miles down the road came to buy some for the half-dozen or so cows that he owned. This neighbor, by most accounts, was a decent person, although it was well known that he and his family were on "public assistance" because he wasn't able to work. I found this to be rather strange since whatever was wrong with him didn't prevent him from hunting and fishing almost daily. I had also observed him carrying 125-lb. deer on his back and 30-lb. stringers of fish several miles, so I was somewhat perplexed.

On the day he came to get the hay, he also had no trouble loading the 50 bales by himself, but after it was loaded, he told my dad that he didn't have the money at that time and, "Would it be okay to pay at the first of the month?" Dad, being the kind-hearted and trusting person that he is, agreed. I was disappointed because I had hoped $7.95 of this hay money could be used to purchase the beloved Timex watch.

On the first of the next month, we expected a huge windfall

of $25 for the hay, but what we got was a visit from the gentleman explaining they had some unexpected expenses come up and it would be the next month before they could pay for the hay. Again, I was disappointed.

When I went to school the next day, however, that disappointment turned to anger when I saw the man's son, who was in the grade below me, wearing a shiny new Timex watch. We eventually got paid later that summer, but I never got the watch. My life was not scarred from never getting the Timex watch, but the impressions were long lasting. The man lived a long life on welfare. So are his sons.

Resourcefulness

I NEVER CEASE TO BE AMAZED at the resourcefulness of most farmers. While some develop these skills out of necessity, most farmers are simply born with that special talent to get things done — one way or another. A look at the "tips and tricks" page of any farm magazine, reading a chapter in *A Million Uses for Baling Wire,* or simply participating in a local educational farm tour should prove to anyone that farmers hold first place in the department of common sense. My father was one of those farmers.

When I was a young boy, not more than nine or ten years old, I was blessed with a most vivid memory of my dad's resourcefulness. That summer, Dad was keeping back several replacement heifers; therefore he had sold the herd bull we had been using for a few years. He was confident that all the cows were bred, so he began to look for a new prospective herd sire. In his mind, there was no need to hire a vet to preg-check the cows, for it had been 21 days since the last cow was in heat.

We found that illusive "perfect bull" 75 miles from home. Although he was just a seven-month-old calf, he had all the makings of a "breed-changer." Dad even shelled out the outrageous asking price of $150, all the time whining to the guy that he had never paid more than a hundred dollars for any mature bull in his lifetime, and never for a bull calf, but dickering proved unsuccessful, so we loaded up the calf and headed for home.

We arrived home late that afternoon, tired and ready to call it a day, but just as we opened the gate to the barn lot, my dad's mouth abruptly dropped open. There, in the middle of the pasture, was a cow in standing heat. Although I didn't have a complete grasp of the birds and the bees yet, I did understand a thing or two about cows and bulls. I knew we had a problem.

In today's agricultural game, AI would be the solution. The problem was, artificial insemination was about as far removed from where I grew up as running water and, as far as Dad was concerned, AI was either the modern-day version of snake oil medicine, or the work of the devil, neither of which he had any use for. Of course, using the neighbors' bulls was out of the question, because they used "white-faced" bulls. Dad always used Angus. In fact, Dad would just as soon not have a calf if it wasn't black. Trouble was, the only Angus bull for miles around was a short, seven-month-old adolescent standing in the back of our pick-up.

After resting his head and arms on the steering wheel for a while, my dad finally raised up and said, "All I know to do ... is to let him out to try." We did.

The little bull knew what he wanted to do, and the cow knew what she wanted done, but their difference in size left both greatly frustrated.

"Go to the shed and get a pick and shovel," Dad commanded me. I was totally confused, but I was old enough to know better than to question my dad.

When I returned with the tools, Dad had the cow in the old milking parlor where four side-by-side stanchions were. We proceeded to dig a large hole about 6-7 feet from the head lock. After the hole was dug, Dad put a little grain in the trough of the stanchion and headed the cow to the feed. Even though the cow had other things on her mind, the smell of the feed lured her in. We locked her head, and her rear feet fit perfectly in our freshly dug pit. We then opened the door to the milking parlor and ran the bull calf in.

That afternoon, the calf became a bull, the cow became pregnant, and I became a believer that any problem can be solved if only you can find a way.

Rain

It was the first day of class for the fall semester of 1993. Missouri had just endured a summer of the worst flooding in this century, with the St. Louis area receiving the worst of it. Sitting before me were 32 juniors and seniors majoring in various areas of agriculture and biology. As I reviewed the student information sheets they had just completed, it was obvious that the majority of these students were from the St. Louis area. With that in mind, I decided to begin this class in "Soil and Water Conservation" by relating its importance to the recent flooding.

"What," I began, "was the single most important factor that contributed to the immense amount of flooding in the St. Louis area this past summer?"

An eager young lady on the front row quickly raised her hand.

"Yes," I said.

"I feel like it was the fault of the Army Corps of Engineers," the young lady replied.

"How so?" I asked.

"I think they have screwed up the building of levees over the past few years, and the result has been misdesigned levees that caused water levels to be too high."

"Interesting," I said.

In the middle of the room, a young man with a pony tail raised his hand to make a comment.

"I doubt that you will agree with me," he began, "but I think farmers are to blame. They are the ones who have plowed up all the land that should never have been farmed, and now all of this tilled land creates too much runoff for the streams and tributaries to handle. That is why there was so much flooding." As the pony-tailed student finished, a third student started speaking without the usual decorum of raising his hand.

"The real reason there was horrendous flooding this past summer," said this neatly dressed young man to my right, "is that the city and county of St. Louis have paved over so much soil with asphalt and concrete that the land simply couldn't absorb the water. That is what led to so much flooding."

By this time I had heard enough. On the back row I saw a young man who had been in one of my classes before. I knew where he was from. He was from a very rural area of Lawrence County, Missouri. With his "Joplin Regional Stockyards" cap sitting low on his brow, he was hoping to avoid eye contact with me, and therefore forced participation in this discussion.

"Joe," I asked, "could you tell the rest of the class why there was so much flooding throughout Missouri this past summer?"

"I believe it rained too damn much," he replied.

"I believe you're right," I said to a surprised but now enlightened class. Life is pretty simple, once you have sense enough to get back to the basics.

Work II

ANGELO AND HIS FAMILY IMMIGRATED to America from Greece sometime during the 1960s. I first became acquainted with him in 1970 when I started eating at his family's steakhouse every Monday evening. As a typically "poor" college student, I took advantage of their Monday "special" — an eight ounce steak with bread, baked potato, salad and drink for a mere $1.69.

Over the years, I have continued to eat at their steakhouse every time I have occasion to return to Columbia. Angelo is always at the grill, taking orders and cooking the steak to perfection. He always has to shake my hand and visit about the latest events in his and my life. Angelo never has to ask me what I want nor how I want it prepared — he knows it by heart. In 27 years of eating there, I have never gotten a bad steak.

The restaurant looks exactly the same as it did in 1970 — the same tables, the same counter, the same signs and the same good food. Even the help is familiar, except that Angelo's siblings have been replaced by his wife, kids, and nephews and nieces. They don't hire many, if any, outsiders to work in the restaurant. Angelo and his family work 12 hours per day, 364 days per year, to make this one of the most successful and profitable restaurants in the country.

A few years ago, I took a group of college students to Columbia to attend a meeting. Naturally, when it was time to eat, I took them to the steakhouse of Angelo's family. In the group was one student who had politely argued with me throughout the year concerning my firm belief that America is still full of opportunity and the American work ethic can still flourish. The student had stated, on many occasions, "only the rich and powerful have opportunity in this country."

It didn't take a Ph.D. in economics to watch the cash register humming along during the evening rush hour to understand how much money was being made that day. "Would you agree this is a very profitable restaurant?" I asked the young doubter. He agreed that it was. I explained to him how the owners came to America , with nothing but a desire to provide a better life for their children and a willingness to do whatever it took to provide that opportunity.

The student finally acknowledged that it was still possible to achieve "the American Dream," but quickly added, "Who, in their right mind, is willing to work that hard to become successful?"

"Successful people," I replied.

Directions

THROUGHOUT MY LIFETIME, I have had several occasions to enter into polite disagreement with leaders in the agricultural industry concerning the background and training of their employees. I have always maintained that people working with and for farmers need to have a basic understanding of production agriculture. Whether they obtain that understanding from experience on the farm or from formal training through some type of agricultural education is not the issue; they must have that *understanding*.

Those who have disagreed with me have countered my assertion with statements like, "The best car salesman I ever knew didn't know the difference between a spark plug and a drain plug," or "You don't have to know where the milk comes from to put it in a gallon jug." Such was the attitude of my friend, Roy.

Roy owned a small meat processing plant near a small town where I used to teach high school agriculture. Roy had developed a profitable little business by hiring unskilled workers at minimum wage and training them to process beef and pork by himself. Most of the workers would move on after a year or two, to meat processors who rewarded their newly obtained skills with higher wages. Roy would then simply hire another and start over. I had tried many times, unsuccessfully, to get Roy to hire some of my graduating seniors who weren't going on to college, but at least had the agricultural background. Roy would always tell me how his employees didn't need to know how the animal grew — just how to kill it and cut it.

Another part of Roy's successful business venture included free pick-up of the animal and delivery of the processed meat. Customers appreciated this service as an important convenience. The new employees had to do it all to learn the trade.

A customer, who was also a friend of mine, called Roy early

one Monday morning to request the pick-up of a steer to have butchered and processed. "You'll find a Holstein steer in a pen on the south side of the barn by my house," he instructed Roy. Roy knew where the customer lived, so he immediately gave the directions to the house and instructions on pick-up to his newest rookie employee.

"What's a Holstein?" the new employee asked.

"It's a black and white calf," Roy replied, "and it should weigh around a thousand pounds."

The new employee grabbed the written directions and took off in the company truck and trailer. The employee found the house without a problem and, sure enough, there was a calf in the pen by the barn. He loaded it. Unfortunately, the calf he loaded was an Angus heifer (with a little white on her underline) on the *NORTH* side of the barn that the customer's son had been caring for to show at the county fair.

When the employee returned, Roy was busy with several customers up front, so the new employee showed the initiative that Roy liked by immediately killing and cutting the newly obtained animal. He was so good that the heifer was already skinned, split and hanging before Roy came back to the kill floor.

Needless to say, Roy had an irate customer later that day; a large bill for a dead purebred heifer; and was the source for many jokes in the community for the next several weeks.

The next time I saw Roy, he said, "I know, I know, you think I should be hiring people who know the difference between a Holstein and an Angus or, at best, the difference between a steer and a heifer."

"Actually, Roy, I was thinking more along the line of someone who knew the difference between the north and the south pen."

Rain, Too

EXPERTS ON HAY QUALITY, even though they disagree on the amount of deterioration, do agree that rain lessens the nutritional value of hay. While I'm no expert, I do know that "rained-on" hay never yields as many bales, and the cattle don't perform as well as they do with good hay. Therefore, farmers will do almost *anything* to get their hay baled and in the barn before a rain falls. In fact, most will pull out all the stops in their race to beat the rain.

Even though God only created economists to make weather forecasters look good, farmers will get so excited when the weatherman predicts rain. Just let the local TV weatherman predict a 90% chance of rain, and you will find farmers — with hay down — doing things that sane people wouldn't do under normal circumstances. I myself have been known to bale hay that I knew wasn't ready to bale, just to beat the rain. I suppose I thought moldy hay would be better than losing those precious nutrients.

Farmers will also "push the edge" on their equipment, running it at speeds for which the machinery wasn't designed, just to get the hay in the barn before a rain. Only last week, a couple I know had hay down. The local weather guru forecasted a "sure chance" of rain with locally heavy storms after midnight. The colorful graphic on the TV screen showed the certainty of the Springfield area getting one or two inches. There was no doubt.

No problem. They started baling at about 4 P.M. By 5 P.M., a rear tire on the tractor went flat. Still no problem. They have a second tractor. By 6 P.M., the radiator on the second tractor sprung a leak. Now, Houston, they had a problem: The rear wheel on the tractor with the bad radiator would not fit the tractor with a flat tire. At 6:30 P.M. in Fair Grove, Missouri, you're not likely to get a flat nor a radiator repaired — at least, not in time to get the hay baled before the dampness of night sets in.

Luckily, in this team of farmers, there was a very creative wife. She drove the pickup to the house, filled every bucket on the place with water and returned to the field. She filled her husband's radiator with water, and he began baling again. As he baled hay, she followed in the truck, stopping every few minutes to add water to the radiator. By dark, they were through. I'm sure that neighbors must have wondered what the heck was going on, but the "can do" spirit of the American farmer prevailed again.

That night it didn't rain. The TV weatherman explained how an odd system had split and went around both sides of the Ozarks. Imagine that.

Fun

THE OTHER DAY, I saw a bumper sticker that read, "I used to have money — now I show horses." Although I don't show horses, my two sons do show cattle, so I can still emphathize with the meaning. My oldest son started showing five years ago, and the youngest joined in three years later. I had been around cattle shows all my life and knew, for most people, there was no money in the venture. But, because of the benefits, I was happy to help get my boys started.

I'm hoping that caring for and showing cattle is teaching my kids plenty of life's necessary qualities. Responsibility, hard work, playing by the rules and accepting defeat are good values for anyone to learn. (They can also learn to catch an unsuspecting victim off-guard with a rubber snake toppling from a barn rafter, or how to delight the eye with the infamous dollar-on-a-string gag ... these, though small, are also important life lessons.) However, for all the virtues of the show barn, the cost of my boys' summer sport and entertainment keeps going up.

We travel anywhere from six to ten local shows each summer, generally one-night, come-as-you-are affairs that don't require a lot of expense and preparation. I like these shows. But we conclude the summer show season with a five-day trip to the Ozark Empire Oven, and while I love the oven, by the fifth day I'm regurgitating whole corn dogs, actually enjoying the cool calf slobber that the barn fans are blowing my way, and more than ready to go home. This year, after our stint at *The Grand New Oven*, I did some rough estimates on just how expensive this "sport" has become for us.

The cost of the heifers varies from year to year, but I assume we can eventually get that back if they live and reproduce. (Their ability to reproduce one year was hampered because I had a bull who had chosen an alternative lifestyle. You learned about that in an earlier chapter.) The tack, feed and show gear can be a tale of woe with grooming chute ($300), blow dryer ($250), halters ($150), grooming supplies ($200), bedding ($150), feed ($500), and miscellaneous ($500 per summer). When you add in entry fees, motel rooms, wear and tear on the truck and trailer, corn dogs, hamburgers, lemonade, pineapple whip, and an obligatory trip to the midway, you're looking at the better part of $3000. As I sat sweltering in the heat of this year's fair, I began to wonder if it was worth it.

Every year, though, when I see a kid win his first trophy or blue ribbon, or simply watch kids and their parents working side by side, I am assured that it is. I guess we'll be back next year doing our part to keep the economy going by spending even more money. As expensive as it is, it's still cheaper than a bass boat, and just as much fun.

Texas Jewels

TOMMY AND HIS WIFE are from East Texas. They, along with their Santa Gertrudis cattle, were stalled directly across the aisle from us at this year's Ozark Empire Fair. We developed an immediate friendship as they were extremely nice people and prone to jokes and laughter that made the heat of the fair more bearable, and they didn't seem to stereotype Texans as having the biggest and best of everything. Tommy is also the first cattleman I've ever met who went out and purchased a fan for himself instead of the cattle. "These Gerts were bred to stand the heat," he said, "but the fat boy needs some wind on his face."

On the first Saturday of the fair, Tommy wanted to attend a Santa Gertrudis sale that was being held south of town. He politely asked if I would take care of their cattle while he and his wife attended the sale. I assured him that I would be happy to pick up after their animals and make sure they were comfortable. "You might keep an eye on the big heifer," Tommy said. "She tends to stretch out when she's sleeping and make her neck tie too tight."

"I'll take care of it," I replied.

"I hate to leave a Yankee in charge, but y'all seem like nice people," he grinned as he walked away. To Tommy, anyone born north of Ft. Worth was a Yankee.

Tommy had been gone about an hour when, sure enough, the big heifer did stretch out for a nap. She laid down in such a manner that all four feet were pointed straight out. The neck tie was tightening, so I decided to wake her before it became a noose. I walked over behind the heifer and slapped her on the rump, but this caused her left rear foot to jerk swiftly backwards and catch me ... well ... slightly below the waist. I doubled over in agony while the rest of the barn doubled over in laughter.

When Tommy returned, he asked how I had made it with his cattle. "I had to wake the big heifer ... once," I said, in a slightly higher voice than before.

"Oh, yeah," he grinned, "I forgot to tell you she's a little goosey when she first wakes up."

"You don't say?" I replied. "I just about lost my masculinity."

"Sorry about that. Pretty painful, huh?"

"Yeah."

Tommy smiled. "Just think how painful it would've been, if you'd been a Texan."

Moo Music

JUST WHEN I BEGAN TO THINK that our government couldn't find any more idiotic ways to waste our money, a story broke last week about cows and music.

It seems that our government funded a research project, to the tune of $500,000, to try to determine if dairy cows would give more milk while being serenaded by music in the barn. Furthermore, if music did aid in increasing milk production, which kind of music would make the cows give the most?

As many of my friends and neighbors are being driven out of the dairy business because of low milk prices, high feed prices and increasingly stringent regulatory requirements slapped on by the same government, it is an especially obscene insult to find out that a half-million of our tax dollars are being spent on such "important" projects as this. I guess it would have made too much sense to have spent that money on research to try and figure out a cheaper way to build adequate lagoons to handle the waste from a dairy facility. Or, better yet, just cut the taxes on dairy farmers by a half-million. Most dairy farmers would probably have liked those results just as well!

As far as the research itself, doesn't our government know that you just can't get anything meaningful out of spending only $500,000. Considering our federal budget (if we could ever get one approved) of one and a half trillion dollars, this cow/music study only cost 33 cents out of every million to conduct. Surely something that insignificant in cost can't be very reliable. To study any subject fairly, it would seem to me that the government would need to spend tens of millions of dollars, wouldn't you agree?

And the results of this study: Cows do give slightly more moo-juice if music is played while they are being milked.

Which kind of music do cows prefer? Mozart seems to induce slightly more milk production than other kinds of music included in this study. But, since the study was limited by small funding,not all kinds of music were able to be bought and compared, so there is obviously a need to have another study in the future that might include music styles such as country, jazz, rap, blues, etc.

I wonder if music style varies between breeds of cows? Do cows prefer different music types between morning and night milking? Is it possible that the cows would like the same music every day or do their tastes change with the seasons? Do the younger cows like the same music as their mothers? My gosh, there is such a need for so many more studies, how shall we ever get all the answers?

Horticulture

My family and I were on our way home from Denver last weekend and happened to stop at a gas station in a remote little town in eastern Colorado. I couldn't help but notice all the yucca plants growing in the pasture that adjoined the service station.

"You know," I began, "lots of people back in Missouri would like to have some of those yucca plants to use in landscaping their yards and businesses."

"Tell them they can have all they want," the station attendant replied. "They're the worst weed we have out here. Nothing will eat them, and the cows won't even eat the grass up next to them."

"Do you suppose these ranchers would let me come out next spring and dig up a trailer load of them for free?" I asked.

"Heck, I know some guys that would pay you to dig up a bunch and haul them off," he answered, as my mind started hearing cash register sounds.

You see, I remembered that some local nurseries get $20-$30 for just one clump of good, green yucca. If I could get some rancher to pay me to dig them, haul them back to Missouri and sell them for even half of what nurseries are getting for them, we're talking some serious green, and I don't mean yucca.

Thinking even farther ahead, while still talking to the guy at the gas station, I tried to think of something I might haul out there to sell so that I would be loaded both ways.

"Do you think homeowners out here in Colorado would be interested in a big, tall, purple-flowered plant for their landscaping needs?" I asked.

"Maybe," he said optimistically.

So, folks ... please don't steal my idea. When springtime rolls around, I'm going to dig up a gooseneck-trailer-load of musk thistle (Missouri's plague of a weed), haul them out to eastern Colorado and sell them to some unsuspecting landscaper. After that deal is done, I'll call on some old rancher and try to get him to pay me to dig a load of yucca and bring it back to Missouri and sell to the homeowners here.

Who would have ever thought there could be so much profit potential in legal weeds!

How Is She Built?

OF ALL THE ADVANCES our society has made during this century, indoor plumbing would have to rank right up there with the microchip, nuclear energy and velcro. Anyone who doesn't agree obviously has never made the trip to the "outhouse" late at night when it's ten below zero ... or raining ... or snowing ... or the batteries in the flashlight were dead.

For the first eight or nine years of my life, we didn't enjoy the convenience of indoor plumbing. Even though those times were thirty-some years ago, I can remember them as if it were just last night, and believe me ... they were NOT the good old days.

As I travel around the Ozarks, I'm surprised by how few outhouses are still standing. When I do see them, I like to make mental notes as to some of their characteristics, for it is these distinguishing points that can tell a lot about the person who lived there. For instance: How far are they from the house? They needed to be close enough for convenience, but far enough away for obvious reasons. Which direction were they located from the house? Most wind is from the northwest in the winter and southwest in the summer. Was it a one-holer, two-holer or bigger? The bigger the family, usually the bigger the outhouse, although it wasn't a place where everyone tried to be at the same time to dry their hair, shave and shower.

When Sears, Roebuck & Co. announced four years ago that they would no longer publish their mail order catalog, most of America was saddened by the passing of a hundred-year tradition. I, on the other hand, found ample reason to celebrate and even found the event worthy enough to hold a party. Of course, most of the people who attended our party had no idea why I wanted to celebrate the end of the catalog era. Those same people who didn't understand wouldn't know the difference between the slick pages and the index.

Some of my friends that I would occasionally spend the night with even used the proverbial corn cobs. So I've been there and done that as well. Corn cobs are the only thing that will make a person thankful for a Sears or Wards catalog. In addition to their roughness, sacks of corn cobs attract mice and rats, which attract black snakes of huge size. This made a lantern or flashlight with good batteries a must for those late-night excursions.

And one other thing ... I didn't find out until just this past year, why it was important to have both white and red corncobs in the sack. Do you know why?

Wood It Make a Difference?

GROWING UP WITH MY BACKSIDE toward a roaring fire in the pot-bellied stove, it didn't take long to learn that nothing warms a home quite like wood heat. My backside wasn't the only thing you could warm with wood heat either. Overshoes and gloves could be strategically placed around the stove so they would be toasty warm when needed.

Not many people heat with wood any more. Oh, there are still lots of homes with fireplaces or inserts for that "homey" feel, but there just aren't many people who rely on wood for their source of heat. Our last home had a wood stove, but when we built a new house seven years ago, my wife thought we should have a cheaper and cleaner source of heat. We chose LP gas. At least it's cleaner.

During one of the recent cold spells, my family visited in the home of a friend who still heats with wood. It was below zero outside, and we were burning up inside. "What kind of wood are you heating with?" I asked.

He replied that "hedge" is the only wood he uses when it is bitterly cold. Ozarks intelligence at its best.

People who have grown up with wood heat don't need a thermal engineer to tell them what kind of wood to use based on the outside temperature. I have seen stoves ruined from the intense heat of burning hedge, from a person who did not know how to use it. Hedge (also known as hedge apple, osage orange and Bois D'Arc) can produce hotter fires than any other wood. Hickory would probably be second in heat produced, with oak coming in third. Other hardwoods would be ranked differently by different authorities, but at the bottom of everyone's list would be elm.

About the only reason anyone would burn elm is to keep a fire going during warm weather, because there certainly isn't going to be much heat produced by burning this timber. Elm just simmers, smolders and smokes ... but no heat. The best description of the heating potential of elm came many years ago from the grandmother of a good friend of mine. She was in her eighties at the time, and someone had given her a pickup load of elm to fire her stove. "I've lived a good life," she began, "and I hope to go to heaven, but if by chance I don't, I can only hope the devil heats with elm."

Education

I'VE NEVER HAD A GREAT DEAL of respect for anyone who isn't willing to put out their maximum effort to get a job done. Yet it seems the willingness to do hard work is a commodity that is increasingly in short supply. I encounter college students every day who think an education or degree of some sort should make them immune from ever having to break a sweat.

Growing up on a farm on the banks of Lick Creek, hard work was never in short supply. Whether it was my parents, most all of our neighbors, or even the kids in the community, there was always hard work to do. Hoeing corn, putting up hay and the daily chores of livestock care kept everyone busy from sunup to sundown every day. And just when we thought we might be caught up with the things that weather and seasons dictate, Dad could find even more things to do, like cleaning out fence rows or painting everything in sight.

As much as I thought I disliked hard work back then, I find that today my favorite activity away from the office is farm work that requires a lot of sweat and great amounts of dirt. People who haven't gone the extra mile to make calluses out of blisters don't know how easy they do have it. My dad still reminds me how easy I have it. In his eyes, the amount of money I make compared to the amount of physical work I do is hard to comprehend.

The best example of the honor in hard work that I can remember happened the week after I graduated from college. I had gone home to stay with my parents for three weeks before my new job started. Mom and Dad were starting to build a new house on some acreage they had just bought after selling the farm. Dad got me out of bed early that Monday morning, and we went out to the building site. Laid out on the hillside were lines where the footing for the foundation should be dug. I assumed we were there to wait on a backhoe to arrive. Wrong.

Dad handed me a pick and said, "Let's get started while we're still in the shade."

"But, Dad," I said only half jokingly, "I have a Bachelor's Degree from the University of Missouri."

My dad stared at me, with raised eyebrows, for what seemed like an eternity. Then in a very serious voice, he said, "Okay, I can show you how to use a pick, but just this one time."

Salesmanship

TO FARM THE HILLS of the Ozarks, and make a living doing it, is to understand the limitations of the land. Unlike more "agriculturally blessed" areas of the U.S., the Ozarks has a shallow and fragile layer of topsoil which makes farming difficult at best. Even the best farmers who relocate here from more fertile regions find it challenging. My father used to say that we Ozarkers could probably make a fortune farming in Iowa, but an Iowa farmer would go broke trying to farm down here.

Back in the early sixties, people from across the country were lured to the Ozarks by cheap land and low taxes (oh, for the good old days). Many were smart enough to farm within the limitations of our geography. Most weren't.

Earl bought a farm up "Possum Walk Creek" from our farm. He was a farmer who had been driven out of California by urban sprawl and the accompanying land prices and taxation. The Ozarks offered the perfect solution to both of these problems — but Earl thought he knew more about how to make a living here than the natives. With big ideas and little knowledge, Earl set out to show the rest of us just what we needed to know.

The first year was kind to Earl. Mother Nature had provided plenty of moisture to supply an abundance of pasture and hay. The second year was more typical of Ozarks' weather patterns. Near the end of Earl's second winter in the Ozarks, he walked in at the local general store where the local spit 'n' whittle club was gathered around the pot-bellied stove. Because of his previous arrogance, Earl had to pull up a nail keg to sit upon while the regulars occupied the benches. Out of feed, out of patience and out of money, Earl despondently asked, "How in the hell have you people been able to make a living around here for all these years?"

One of our neighbors shifted his pipe to the corner of his

mouth, nodded and replied, "I know a few old boys that have made a pretty good living selling land to Californians, and then buying it back a couple years later for about fifty cents on the dollar. Shall I tell them you're ready to sell?"

Nobody ever knew where Earl moved after he sold his place.

Decontamination

AGRICULTURAL NEWS BECAME consumer news last week when 25 million pounds of hamburger meat were recalled by one of the nation's largest meat processors. The meat was recalled because of *possible* contamination by a potentially deadly bacteria. Being a consumer, as well as a producer of beef, I felt good that our system of food inspection had caught this problem before the masses became sick. But I couldn't help wondering why I didn't die as a child.

Every Sunday morning of my childhood, Dad or Mom would go to the chicken house and catch the noon meal. They would take the chicken to the old block of wood (that was stained with the blood of hundreds of Sunday meals before), take a rusty ax and chop off the head of the fowl. The headless chicken would then flop around on the dirty ground for a few seconds before it was plucked, gutted and cut up to fry. It was good.

There was also the annual autumn ritual of hog-killin'. Friends and neighbors would gather at our farm to ensure the winter's meat supply by processing a couple of 250-lb. hogs. The "sanitary" processing included scalding the carcass in a rusty 55-gallon barrel (that probably once contained something poisonous), laying the carcass on some old wooden planks, in order to cut it up with that same rusty ax and an old handsaw that Dad retained just for this job. There had to be some bacteria somewhere, but it was delicious.

I've been inside modern meat processing plants. There is absolutely no comparison between them and the primitive ways we used to handle meat. Today, meat plants are the epitome of cleanliness and sanitation — so why didn't I die or at least get sick as a child?

Answer: Mom *cooked* the meat!

Mom's fried chicken was done. Through and through. The ham was fried until it was the texture of jerky, but was it great!

There was no such thing as "rare" steak. Well done was your only selection.

With today's trendy orders of raw fish, barely cooked steaks and "squishy" chicken, I'm surprised the entire population hasn't come down with some disease associated with undercooked food.

In the meantime, I was hoping that meat company would give us, free of charge, some of that tainted meat. I believe Mom could cook it to safety.

Thistles

RARELY, IF EVER, can you get *all* farmers to agree on anything. This past spring and summer was different, however, for *every* farmer I've visited with in the past five months has agreed that this is the worst year ever for trying to control the thistle problem on their land. It seems that both musk thistle and Canadian thistle have never been worse. I agree.

After wearing out three garden hoes, two hand-held pump sprayers and a wife, I started taking notes on innovative methods of weed control that my friends and neighbors were utilizing.

One friend waited until the windiest day after the seed heads of the thistle were fully bloomed, then bush-hogged the field. He insisted that 99% of the seeds left his land. Unfortunately, his upwind neighbor used the same control method. More unfortunately, I live downwind from both of them.

Another friend imported some of those foreign beetles to eat the thistle on his place. The beetles weren't working fast enough, so he put 75 cows on the 15-acre patch of thistles for the entire month of July. According to him, "If cows get hungry enough, they'll eat anything." He only lost seven head.

Yet another friend resorted to digging the thistles, potting them and tried to sell them to homeowners as a flowering perennial. He was arrested by the Department of Agriculture for transporting prohibited weeds across state lines, even though several people commented on "how beautiful the flowers were."

I didn't attempt any of those methods, but I do finally have my thistle problem under control, and it happened quite by accident. The solution to the thistle problem — overgraze your pasture during the July drought; then after the bountiful rains during August your ragweed will grow so fast it will choke out the thistle.

Now, if I could only get rid of the ragweed.

Bargains

IT WOULD SEEM that paving companies have great difficulty in figuring the exact number of truckloads of asphalt it takes to complete a job, thus leaving them with one or two truckloads left over. They, in turn, want to sell the leftover asphalt to someone "far below their cost" because ... well, they can't take it back.

I must admit the first time I was approached with this sales technique, some 20 years ago, and at least 15 times since, I actually believed that there was a legitimate overestimation of materials and thought I could possibly get the "bargain of a lifetime" by taking advantage of the situation. But after adhering to the old adage that if something sounds too good to be true, it probably is, and checking out some prices, I found this sales technique to be just that — a great sales technique, and one more of us ought to take advantage of.

The dairy farmer could bottle up a few gallons of fresh milk and hit the road. Making his first call, he could walk up to the unsuspecting patron's door and say, "My cows produced so much milk today that the milk truck couldn't haul it all. It will surely spoil before the milk truck returns, so instead of dumping it down the drain, I thought you might want it for $2.50 a gallon." (Cheaper than in the store, but twice what the farmer normally gets.)

I myself intend to load a couple of feeder calves in the trailer and head out on the door-to-door route. I've already got my sales pitch memorized:

"Good afternoon, sir. This is a lovely place you have here. I just brought a load of calves down to the auction barn, and it seems they didn't have room to accept all of them. Instead of wasting money hauling them back home, I thought you might want to buy them for a discounted price of only $600 each. Calves grazing out in your back yard would surely make your place look prettier, and you'd never have to mow your lawn again."

You would be able to sell to a limitless number of people. Of course, I'll probably have the best luck where I see a newly paved driveway.

Emus

FARMERS AND RANCHERS KNOW what to do when a calf gets out of the pen. It usually involves a rope, maybe a horse, possibly a pickup truck, and quite likely several people, unless a good stock dog is handy. But, as agriculture changes and new species of "livestock" become commonplace, the old methods of "cowboying" may not work so well.

Wade (not his real name) is a farmer. He also works for the Ozark Empire Fair. During last week's Farmfest at the fairgrounds, Wade was put in charge of capturing an emu that had escaped from his display pen. While Wade wouldn't have had a problem capturing a runaway calf, cow or bull, the emu roundup became quite a spectacle.

According to Wade, emus can neither be roped, because they can run right through a loop, nor can they be "bulldogged" from a speeding golf cart, since the emu can contort its neck in any position imaginable, leaving the cowboy to grab nothing more than thin air.

After the chase had lasted some 45 minutes and reaching speeds of up to 30 MPH, the emu was cornered on the slick concrete surface of one of the open-air eating areas of the fair grounds. Because emus have trouble keeping their footing on slick surfaces, the bird fell. Wade, with lightning quickness, pounced on the downed fowl, knocking the wind out of them both. He quickly wrapped one arm around the bird's body while he desperately tried to grab the neck with his other hand. It looked like a fireman trying to straddle the middle of a high-pressure water hose.

The other 15 people who had been involved in the emu capture cheered wildly as Wade lay there with one arm around the bird's body and the other hand gripping the emu's neck, a neck that now resembled a wriggling rattlesnake. Wade, with a big smile and sweaty face, acknowledged their applause. His smile quickly disappeared though, as he looked toward the nearest spectator and said, "Please tell me this emu is a female and that's an egg pressing against my right arm."

"Nope," replied the co-worker, "I'm afraid it's not."

Marketing

ALFALFA HAS LONG BEEN a lucrative cash crop for farmers across the Midwest. It consistently ranks in the top three cash crops for Missouri farmers and is one of the few high-income crops that can be produced successfully here in the Ozarks. One of the great things about alfalfa is that it can very easily attain added value, depending on how it is marketed and who it is marketed to.

For example, a normal bale of quality alfalfa hay, sold to a beef cattleman, might be worth $3 per bale. Alfalfa is generally considered "too good" to feed to beef cattle since they can survive quite well on lower quality hay with less protein content. That same bale of alfalfa might sell to a dairy farmer for $4 per bale because dairy cows need that extra protein for milk production. Horse owners would be willing to pay $5 per bale because they want those high-dollar horses to have the very best, and well ... they're horse people.

At the same time, that same bale of alfalfa hay can be dehydrated, put in a plastic bag labeled with a prestigious feed company logo, and sold to whomever for $7 per bale. If the feed company has the equipment to convert the raw hay into cubes or pellets for feed additives, the single bale of hay might then be worth $10. It keeps increasing in value based entirely on processing and marketing.

In 1970, I observed two farm boys who got the most money for alfalfa hay that I've ever seen. The two young men were roommates at college, both majoring in agriculture and living on a dormitory wing that was dominated by "aggies." There were, however, a couple of "tie-dyed types" that also lived there. The one who always wore a headband approached the two Ozark farm boys to see if they could get some "Ozarks-gold" on their next trip home. The aggies quickly looked at each other, smiled and nodded.

When the two farm boys went home that next weekend, they proceeded to grind and chop a combination of alfalfa hay and oak leaves into a burnable mixture. The aggies then sold the two-ounce bag to the young men for $10. That figures out to be approximately $4800 per bale for alfalfa hay.

It's all in how you market your product.

Murder or Self-Defense

HER LIFE WAS SNUFFED OUT in one tragic night. Her potential would never be realized. Her only legacy was the son left behind ... the son that she had given birth to only four short months before.

Some called it an unfortunate accident, while others saw it as a clear case of murder. Whichever it was, I didn't enjoy my role in providing "expert" testimony this past week, in a trial that would eventually establish guilt or innocence. On the witness stand, before me, were graphic pictures of the scene — the victim with her broken neck, awkwardly disfigured as she lay dead. Lying beside her was the accused — his bloody head and mangled leg were obvious proof that something horrendous had taken place during that hot, starlit summer night seven years ago.

The attorneys argued while the judge listened patiently. Both sides had agreed to waive their right to a trial by jury, so the eventual decision lay in the hands of the Solomon-like judge. With one lawyer acting like Johnny Cochran and the other one Marsha Clark, I felt more like Kato than an expert witness (come to think of it, the bearded justice even resembled Judge Ito). The lawyers paced back and forth as they thoughtfully probed every possible angle. The drama and tension mounted as they sought their version of the truth or, at the very least, justice.

"Do you think this unfortunate accident could have been prevented?" asked one attorney.

"Yes," I replied.

"How?"

"If the bull had been secured with his nose ring," I answered.

With all the theatrics of this courtroom drama, it was easy for them — and me — to forget that the case revolved around a cow that was killed by a bull while they were both tied outside at a local county fair in 1990. The owner of the cow was simply trying to get the insurance company to pay for the worth of his cow. But ... for a brief time that day, we were all involved in the "trial of the century."

Environmentalists

I ADMIT THAT I'm usually more than a little skeptical when I browse through the aisles of my local grocery store and observe all the "environmentally friendly" products that are now for sale. Now don't get me wrong — I'm all for keeping our world as clean and unpolluted as we can, even though I still cringe every time I lick the seal on an envelope touting "made from recycled products." *But come on,* a plastic that will rot in 500 years as opposed to the normal 600 years can only be playing to a sympathetic public that will buy *anything t*hat is a member of the "green squad." People feel good if they *believe* their actions will help the environment. Just ask Halbert.

Halbert grew up deep in the Ozark Hills of southern Missouri. Other than a family trip to Arkansas and his attendance at the University, Halbert had never been very far from the hills. But this all changed in 1974 when he decided to take a college travel course that allowed him to tour the highlights of European agriculture. As excited and apprehensive as he was, Halbert never realized that the most interesting part of his trip would happen in New York City.

A three-hour layover at New York's Kennedy Airport found Halbert and his classmates killing time by relaxing around one of the many passenger waiting areas. Halbert began to get a strange feeling that someone was watching him, so he turned around to see a middle-aged woman sitting a couple of seats to his right, staring at his cowboy boots. She kept staring and staring in the direction of his feet. Feeling a bit uncomfortable, Halbert asked, "Can I help you, ma'am?"

A distinctly New York accent shot back, "What kinda shoes AW doze?"

"They're cowboy boots, ma'am," Halbert replied.

"Why on uth would you wunna wayah doze pointy-toed things?" she said with a cocked finger pointed straight at his boots.

"Well, ma'am," he began, "I'm a real cowboy, and real cowboys have to use horses a lot to take care of their cows. These here 'pointy-toed' boots fit real nicely in the stirrup of a saddle and ain't as likely to get hung up in that stirrup since they got these high heels." The lady wrinkled her brow. Halbert continued. "The tops are high so my legs don't get all scraped up when I ride through the brush, plus it takes a lot more leather to make boots than shoes which helps keep the price up on the cattle I produce."

The woman, still not convinced, pondered the logic behind Halbert's words. He then went for the knockout punch.

With voice and expression convincing enough to belie his future profession of minister, Halbert went for the "green."

"Ma'am, we've also got a real bad cockroach problem back on the ranch. So many cockroaches, it just ain't safe with all the diseases and germs they carry. Why, with these pointy-toed boots, we can just run them suckers into a corner and squash 'em without havin' to use a bunch of poisons and chemicals that could hurt the environment, you know. With all due respect, ma'am, you couldn't kill anything in a corner with those round-toed shoes you're wearin'."

She shook her head. "I am so sawry," she said, "I had no idea how impawtant they wuh." She was now a believer in the environmental necessity of the cowboy boot.

I'm still waiting for my favorite bootmaker to come out with a box stamped "environmentally friendly." It's just a matter of time.

Time

I AM A CREATURE OF HABIT. I always have been. Most of the time, with the exception of getting on the nerves of my wife and sons, it has always worked to my advantage. I get up at the same time every morning; I go through the same routines of personal hygiene; I perform the daily chores in a manner as such that my friends and family always know where I am, based solely upon the time of the day. But, twice per year, my orderly life becomes screwed up.

One of my life-long dreams has been to meet the person, or persons, who came up with the idea of *Daylight Savings Time*. I would like for them to spend the first few days of each time change working side by side with a farmer. Had they been with me last Sunday morning, they could have witnessed the fiasco that was the first day of Central Standard Time at the Crownover farm.

As usual, I arose at 6:30 A.M. (I had remembered to reset the alarm clock the night before so that it was now 7:30, old time). I'm usually at the barn by 7 A.M., but that was delayed 30 minutes because I had to reset all the clocks in the house. My wrist watch and the clock-radio were no problem. I even mastered the clock on the microwave and coffee pot with great success. The clocks in the truck and car required me to read the owner's manuals, but after no more than 10 minutes they were reading the new time as well. The time on the TV required me to look in both the owner's manual *and* the dictionary. A long time ago, I conceded victory to the VCR and simply allow it to flash 12:00, year 'round.

By the time I made it to the barn, I was now (according to the animals' internal clock) an hour and a half late. The barn cats were the first to display their displeasure by bringing blood. One scratched my arm as I entered the feed sack. I was also victim to the bull that I keep in the barn during fall calving season. Normally very gentle, he butted the feed bucket out of my hand, scattering grain everywhere, letting me know that he, too, didn't appreciate my late hour. I could only imagine what dairymen were going through.

Within a couple of weeks, both I and the livestock will be conditioned to the new time and everyone will be happy again — that is, until next April.

Solvency

As THE LAST OF AUGUST rolls around, I find myself having mixed emotions with school starting. This is the first time, since 1958, that I haven't been in school either as a student or as a teacher. Part of me is relieved while another part misses the excitement of a new school year. In order to help me make the transition from teacher to farmer, I've decided to run my farm like a school.

I'll be the superintendent. Since I've always wanted to have that kind of power and own the place — I can do that. I'll need a good principal, though, to oversee all the day-to-day stuff and do the work I dislike (not to mention having someone to blame if it all goes wrong). I'll need a support staff also: A nutritionist to oversee the proper feeding of the livestock; a nurse to make sure sick and injured cattle receive proper care; an athletic director to train and prepare the better cattle for show; a transportation director to coordinate timely shipping and receiving of cattle onto the farm; a compliance officer to make sure the farm operates within all the rules and guidelines of the USDA, DNR, EPA, OSHA and a bunch of other government bureaucracies; plus custodians and secretaries to keep the farm clean and running efficiently.

I also have some inventive ideas on how to improve productivity on the farm. First, I plan to implement a program of "cow tenure." Once any cow has produced five calves for me, she will be automatically tenured and guaranteed a place to live out her life as long as she doesn't eat some loco weed or kick the superintendent.

Secondly, I'll test every calf every year. If this year's calves don't perform as well as last year's, I'll have my counselor (whoops, there's another person to hire) write a grant to the USDA for funding to find out why they didn't weigh as much.

Lastly, I'll make sure my equal opportunity officer (my gosh, there's yet another position to fill) assures equal numbers of black, white and red cows on the farm. I'll also let the equal opportunity officer conduct all of the artificial insemination so that we never have to hire another male (bull) as long as the farm exists.

On second thought, if I want to keep farming for a while, maybe I had better run my farm like a farm.

Foreigners

DEER SEASON IN OZARK COUNTY was a special time back in the early 1960s. It was a time for the locals to bag that trophy buck on the "back 40" in a manner legal enough to brag to their neighbors and have their picture taken for the *Ozark County Times*. It was also a time, long before managed game ranches, when farmers could earn a few extra dollars by allowing hunters from the big city to hunt on their property.

Dad was always happy to let hunters from Springfield pay him a small fee to hunt on our farm because, as he put it, "Most of the guys from Springfield have grown up in the country and know what they're shooting at." He was a little more reluctant to let men from Kansas City hunt on our place, but most were pretty responsible and he usually let them hunt as well. St. Louis hunters were a different story, though. I don't know whether St. Louisans had never seen a deer before they arrived in Ozark County, or whether they had simply imbibed too much of their city's most famous brew, but there seemed to be a problem most every year.

One of our neighbors, who always maintained a good number of brush goats, lost one or two every deer season to a gunshot wound right behind the front shoulder. Another neighbor who milked Jerseys kept the calves in the barn during deer season and, after several unfortunate incidents, even resorted to writing the word "COW," in red paint, on both sides of each of his animals for the week of deer season — just in case the hunters from St. Louis had never seen a Jersey either.

Alas, not all St. Louis hunters killed goats and cattle. As a matter of fact, the most famous deer kill in Ozark County came at the hands of a skilled St. Louis hunter. As soon as the pickup pulled into the check station, a crowd gathered quickly to look at the huge animal laying in the bed of the truck. The game warden came over to see what the commotion was all about and was shocked to see what was before him.

"Whatta ya got there?" he asked the proud hunter.

"I got myself a mule deer," the smiling marksman answered. "It took three of us to load him in the truck, and I didn't even know there were mule deer down here."

"He's a big one all right," the game warden continued. "Where'd you kill him?"

"Up on Mr. Jones' place, just off Highway 5. I only paid twenty dollars to hunt there this year."

"If I were you, I'd volunteer to come back next summer and plow Mr. Jones' garden," quipped the game warden.

"Why?" asked the hunter.

"Because you've just killed the burro that Mr. Jones uses to plow."

It must have been a long trip back to St. Louis.

Sale Barn

WHEN I WAS A KID, nothing gave me greater pleasure than to accompany my father on his weekly trips to the "sale barn." Everything about the livestock auction was intriguing to me — from the chant of the auctioneer — to the order buyers (whom my dad referred to as "gamblers," but a necessary evil) who were spending thousands of someone else's dollars ... to the ringmen who could make their leather whips sound like a 12-gauge shotgun. Wearing $20 hats and $50 boots, these men were my idols. While other kids looked up to Mickey Mantle and Willie Mays, I wanted to be the sale barn owner who could stand in the same ring with a crazed cow and calmly set her starting price by yelling, "Thuty-five!"

A lot has changed at the sale barn over the years. My last visit to a new, ultra high-tech auction barn found big-screen TVs blaring out the latest country music videos prior to the start of the sale. The sale barn owner sat in the safety and cleanliness of the auctioneer's booth as he set the starting price. No skill in guessing the weight of the cattle is needed any more, since the weight is flashed on electronic panels or closed circuit TVs as the animals sell. The leather whips have been traded in on large plastic instruments that resemble oversized fly swats that make a disappointing thud (no doubt to appease the animal rights groups). The auctioneer still chants, but seems more difficult to understand as he tries to sell 500-600 head per hour.

I was also amazed to see a couple of the major buyers sitting behind laptop computers, plugged into one of many telephone outlets scattered throughout the auditorium. I suspected they were on the Internet, monitoring the commodity market as they decided how many to buy or how much to pay. Being a curious sort, I discreetly moved over behind one of the computer-operating buyers to a position at which I could see what was on the screen. I saw no quotes for fat cattle at Omaha, nor feeder cattle at Oklahoma City, but only the latest betting line ... for the NFL ... from Las Vegas.

Oh well, it was nice to see that some things don't change.

Good Farmers

ONE OF MY STUDENTS recently returned from a trip abroad where he had worked on a farm in Switzerland for a few months. As he made a presentation to my class, I found it very interesting that the Swiss farmer he had lived with required my student to comb out the tails of the milk cows each morning before turning them out to pasture. The student went on to explain that this was important to the farmer, for the people of Switzerland could tell the "good farmers" by the cleanliness and appearance of the cows' tails.

This story made me begin thinking about the habits and customs of American farmers that prove to their neighbors that they are, indeed, "good farmers." For instance, I can remember many hot summer afternoons spent with a brush-hook cleaning the sprouts, poke stalks and multi-flora rose out of the fence rows. To my dad, a clean fence row was a source of pride and ample evidence that he was a good farmer. To older crop farmers that I have known, the ultimate of compliments was the fact that people would recognize that their rows were the straightest in two counties. Fat cows toward the end of winter, board fences that received an annual white-washing, well-braced corner posts and weedless fields are just a few of the many ways that farmers make a statement that they are the "best" at what they do.

I also remember visiting with a wonderful old farmer in northern Missouri a few years ago. A friend and I were hunting deer on his land one autumn weekend during the early 1980s. As we visited at his shop after an unsuccessful hunt, he commented, "Things are so good you can't tell the good farmers from the bad ones, because they are all driving new 1982 pickups." The same farmer, three years later, reminded me that, "Things are so bad, you can't tell the good farmers from the bad ones, because they are still driving the same 1982 pickups."

In my part of the country, it might be difficult to identify the good farmers from the bad ones. If you consider the past few years have seen the floods of '93, the drought of '95 (which continued into '96), the lowest beef prices since I was a kid, and the highest feed prices EVER, I suppose the good farmers are the ones that are still farming ... those that look forward, once again, to the newborn calves of spring ... to the potential of a bumper crop ... to prospering at the life they love.

In the meantime, I think I'll send my two sons down the south fence row with my dad's old brush-hook.

Meaning What?

THERE WAS A TIME when people read and obeyed the signs or labels that warned of dangers, reasons to be cautious, or simple rules to follow. That doesn't seem to be the case any more. In fact, you're just as likely to hear someone say, "I didn't see the sign," or "I didn't know that applied to me."

Much of the disregard probably has something to do with the way the command is worded — or maybe it's related to the sheer number of signs we all have to deal with that has made us a little numb to the consequences of disobedience. In just the past couple of weeks I have observed people smoking directly in front of "No Smoking" signs on three separate occasions. I have also been amused at tobacco chewers, at a sale barn where "No Spitting" signs are placed everywhere, continue to chew and spit on the floor. On the other hand, I have been nearly licked to death by a dog in the yard with a "Dangerous Dog" sign.

I have, however, talked to people who seem to have the problem solved. A business owner, who was having problems with theft by night-time trespassers, erected a large sign that stated, "Trespassers will be shot — survivors will be prosecuted." The trespassing problem was virtually eliminated. Another business owner was having a real problem with people filling up his trash bin with personal trash. He installed surveillance cameras and a sign that read, "Smile as you dump your trash — you're being video-taped by hidden cameras." Problem solved. After years of problems with people fishing my ponds without permission, I have even been successful by installing a sign that says, "Caution, fish in this pond are contaminated with the deadly poison — Dioxin." It works. I just hope the EPA doesn't take me serious.

But in order for all the signs and labels to work, we must say what we mean and mean what we say. Just last week, one of the many parcel delivery companies arrived at my house with two packages. The package for my wife contained some pharmaceutical kits. The package was not labeled "Fragile" even though the contents were very much so. Many of the vials arrived broken.

Attached to the package for me were no less than four labels declaring it "Fragile, Breakable, and Handle with Care." Inside were two 3/4-inch hardened-steel bolts for the tractor. My best guess is that the box with the vials of medicine was thrown against the "fragile" bolts during shipment.

Oh, by the way, the bolts weren't hurt at all.

Hats

NOT MANY PEOPLE WEAR HATS any more. Oh, sure, everybody and their dogs wear caps, but I'm talking about hats ... with a crown and a brim and a significant amount of money invested; an item of headwear that can tell you a lot about the person wearing it.

People who wear hats every day wear the same basic style of hat their entire life. They also wear it the same way, whether it is tilted to one side, or back on their head, or however. This consistency in style and method tells me that this person is stable, reliable, and most likely an honest individual.

Politicians rarely wear hats any more.

Harry Truman wore a hat. The fact that he once owned a hat store probably had something to do with it, but nonetheless, Harry knew how to wear a hat. In every picture I've ever seen of the man, his hat was always worn the same. It also looked like a good quality hat, and even though he was a Democrat, I think I would have been inclined to vote for him, had I been around in that era.

Lyndon Johnson wore a hat, but it never looked the same on him from day to day. Most Texans I've known throughout life knew how to wear a hat because they grew up wearing one. But not LBJ.

Ronald Reagan was the last President to regularly wear a hat. Mr. Reagan wore the same kind of hat, the same way, the same style every time. I admire that in a man.

Last week I saw one of the presidential candidates wearing a hat while trying to woo the voters of a Western state. You could tell it was the first time he had ever worn a hat because it looked awkward on him. The hat was shaped funny, like it had just come out of a box that was damaged in shipment. It was also black, and everyone knows that good guys wear white hats. Bad choice.

The other day, as I was following a pickup truck down the highway, I noticed the driver was wearing a hat. It was pulled down low on his forehead and had a short crown and narrow brim. Because of the hat and the way he wore it, I knew it had to be an old friend that I hadn't seen in several years. As I passed him on the interstate, I saw that it was the old friend and waved.

It would be nice if we could still identify old friends and good politicians by the hats they wear.

Trading

I USED TO ASSUME that everyone knew how to play the "trading game," but I have since learned that this art is one that is either despised or avoided by a large percentage of the general population. Personally, I have always enjoyed the challenge of attaining the lowest price on items such as automobiles, furniture, major appliances, anything advertised in the classified ads, or even a good pair of boots. However, I have friends that even go to that new kind of car dealer, where everyone pays the sticker price, just to avoid the negotiating hassle. Sorry, but I need that sticker price that's jacked up sky high so I can get them to come down $3000 in order to feel like I got a great deal.

A couple of weeks ago I took both my sons with me when I went to trade trucks. It wasn't so much that I wanted to impress them with my trading ability (for it's not all that great), but I did want them to begin to understand "how" to trade and negotiate on price. After all, I learned by watching my dad, and I'm quite sure he learned by watching his father.

I tried to teach the boys a few of the finer points of trading, such as:

(A) Never be in a hurry to trade. If you can reach the compromise price in one day, you can rest assured that you probably paid too much.

(B) Get at least two dealers working against each other. They love to think they are taking business away from their competitors.

C) Always act like you hate to give up your old vehicle. Even though it barely got you there and you can't wait until someone else is stuck with the old heap and the daily repairs that accompany it, act like it's a member of the family.

On the way home from making the deal, both boys expressed embarrassment that I acted like some old, frugal tightwad. I had to remind them that no salesman has ever sold a new vehicle for less than it cost them. I expect the salesman to make money on the deal; I just don't want them to make their whole week's commission out of my one trade. This explanation seemed to satisfy them.

Hopefully, my sons will grow up to be less naive about trading than their mother was when I first met her. We had been dating for a few months when she asked me to go to a furniture store with her to purchase a new bedroom set she had been wanting. When she found the set she wanted, she asked the salesman how much it would cost. He indicated that it would cost $1249.

"Isn't that a shame," I said, "you only have a thousand dollars to spend, don't you?"

I realized Judy didn't know how to play the game when she looked at me funny and said, "No, I have that much."

Parents and Teachers

IT'S TIME ONCE AGAIN for schools to start all over the Ozarks. The newspaper and television stories have already started about low test scores, lack of money, student violence, and on and on. What can be done? I certainly don't profess to have the answers to these problems, but I can draw upon my own experiences in education to challenge teachers, administrators and parents.

My first five years of school (without the benefit of preschool or kindergarten) were in a one-room schoolhouse at Mammoth. Mrs. Evelyn Morrison was my teacher for the first and second grade. She taught all eight grades under one roof, and I think there were about 20 of us. Mrs. Pamela Trump was my teacher for the next three years after some minor consolidation which led to only three grades at Mammoth. There were six light bulbs in the building, but no phones, faxes, computers nor copy machines. We drew the drinking water each morning from a hand pump in front of the building. There was no school breakfast nor lunch program. In the winter, heat was provided by a wood stove in the center of the classroom. Wood was provided free of charge by the parents. There was no organized sports teams, no gym, and students had to buy their own paper and pencils. And yes, I did have to walk to school.

I relate all of these things to remind you that times have never been great for schools. But most of us succeeded in spite of the needs. Those two teachers were excellent and cared about the success of their students. They knew our parents, where each of us lived, and what kind of resources we had. They were demanding and made the best of what they had to work with there at school.

Good teachers are very important, and nice buildings help out, too, but the bottom line is that parents are the most important ingredient in a quality education. At Mammoth, I knew that if I got into trouble, the whipping I got at school would pale in comparison to the one I would get when I got home. Parents can't put their kids on the bus next week and expect the school to transport, feed, educate, discipline, clothe and otherwise raise their sons and daughters. Schools shouldn't have to be the source of their knowledge about drugs, sex, morality and ethics. Parents have the responsibility for the real education of their children. Schools need to concentrate on the academics.

We don't need longer school days nor longer school years. We do need to spend the seven hours per day in getting the most out of those students from an academic standpoint. We need homework, and we need parents to enforce that homework and get involved in the education process.

Those of us who went to little one-room schools like Mammoth, Faye, Howard's Ridge, Center Point, and all the rest, certainly didn't have highly paid teachers and lavish school buildings. Most all of us, however, had two parents who wanted to know what had gone on at school that day, and what we had to do that night.

Teachers need to do their job to the best of their ability. Parents need to recognize they have a job to do that is every bit, if not more, as important as the teacher's.

Pitchforks and Teats

ONE COLD WINTER MORNING, back in 1972, my college chemistry professor began class as usual ... with a question. "What is the coldest substance known to mankind?" he asked.

Since I wasn't very bright in the area of chemistry, I hadn't gotten the chance to answer many of his questions, but that one was just too easy. "A pitchfork handle on a ten-below-zero morning," I proudly replied.

The professor belittled me in front of the entire class by stating, "Anyone who has even the most basic understanding of chemical elements would know that liquid nitrogen is the coldest substance."

As the rest of the class laughed, I thought to myself, "Anyone who has ever had to feed hay on a ten-below-zero morning knows better."

We were one of the last farmers in the world to convert over to baling hay. For most of my childhood years, we put up loose hay, which meant we had to handle all the hay with pitchforks. It didn't matter what kind of gloves were worn — soft brown jersey, yellow fuzzy chore or leather work gloves — the internal temperature of a pitchfork handle would literally freeze a person's hands in a matter of only a few minutes.

About the only way you could convince your mind to endure this intense cold was to tell yourself that in a few short minutes your hands would come in contact with the warmest substance known to mankind — a cow's teat on a ten-below-zero morning. For once you had forked enough hay into the manger, you could climb down from the loft, yank those gloves off, and start milking ol' Bossy. Feeling the steam coming off that warm milk, exercising cold and stiff fingers and simply absorbing the heat from the cow's teats was relief beyond description.

If ol' Bossy could have talked, I wonder what answer she would have given as the coldest substance on earth?

Professors

I RECEIVED SEVERAL of those new-fangled "Christmas Letters" this past holiday season. Now that a majority of the population has a home computer, it's easy for people to personalize their letters by making the first paragraph relate to the receiver, and the remainder of the information about the sender and their family and what happened to them over the last year — much like a mass mailing of junk mail, but I like it.

One of the letters that I received was from a former professor. This dear old friend was the best teacher I had in my 20 years of education. He is an intellectual who can quote everyone from Shakespeare to Will Rogers, but amazingly has a great deal of common sense as well. I first met Glen, who is a native "Okie," while I was an undergraduate at the University of Missouri. From there, he moved to Mississippi State University, where I went for my graduate degree. Glen was my major professor at MSU and, other than my parents, had more influence on my adult life than anyone else. As a student, I always tried my best to live up to his expectations. Many times, however, I'm sure I let him down.

One of those times was when I presented him with the first draft of my thesis proposal. The proposal was 25 pages long (by far, the longest paper I had ever written), and I had spent a month making sure it was the best I could do. When Glen returned it to me a week later, I was certain he had used up at least three red-ink pens. I could hardly read what was not marked out or corrected. At the bottom of the last page, Glen wrote, "It is obvious to the reader that you're from the Ozarks, and the schools you've attended up to now have been inadequate in grammar instruction. Don't get discouraged because I have confidence that you can overcome this handicap."

I was devastated.

Glen is now a department head and professor at Texas A&M University, arguably one of the most prestigious agricultural colleges in the country. While reading through Glen's Christmas letter, I couldn't help but notice at least ten errors in grammar, punctuation and spelling. I was compelled to circle the errors in red ink and return the letter to him with this comment at the bottom of the page: "It is obvious to the reader that you are from Oklahoma and the school at which you now teach is inadequate in grammar instruction. Don't get discouraged because I have confidence that you can overcome this handicap."

I just hope Glen was able to see the humor.

Support Groups

WHILE BROWSING THROUGH the Sunday paper last week, I noticed an entire page devoted to the meeting times and places of a vast number of "support groups" for adults. Many of them, undoubtedly, serve a valuable cause. Groups like **Mothers Against Drunk Driving** and **Alcoholics Anonymous** have long helped many people and do provide important services to their members. Others seem ... well, a bit odd to me.

Support groups for those "addicted to sex and love" would seem to be a stretch for me. The meeting time and place was **NOT** listed for this group, as I'm sure many single men would find this a haven for picking up any women in attendance. The support group for "heterosexual cross-dressers" also caught my attention. Can there be that many attendees here in Southwest Missouri?

An entire page of listings would make one think that every possible support group for every possible addiction and affliction would be covered. But not so. I've come up with my own list of support groups that I would be interested in attending, yet none of these were listed. I've even come up with good meeting places and times I think would be appropriate.

Support Group for Men Addicted to Farming — a group designed to help men work through their unnatural addiction to an unpredictable and, most of the time, unprofitable occupation. Meets every spring at the Las Vegas Convention Center.

Support Group for Conservative Republican College Professors —Meets weekly in the phone booth at the Campus Union. That should be plenty of room for both of us.

Support Group for People who feel Over-Taxed — Meets every April 15 at the home of their congressman. Come prepared to stay a while, until the congressman returns from his latest junket to some exotic vacation spot.

Support Group for Parents of Teenage Kids Addicted to Rock Music — Meets weekly at the city park. Sign language will be provided for the hearing-impaired. No musical talent required.

Support Group for Owners of "Lemon" Automobiles — Meets daily at the local garage. Taxi service will be provided.

I had many more identified yesterday, but I've forgotten them. Guess I'd better attend the meeting for the "support group for forgetful people."

Solicitation

I MAY HAVE FOUND A WAY to get rid of those unwanted telephone solicitors that always call at the worst possible times during the evening hours. These calls have always annoyed me, but since I get no great pleasure out of being rude to anyone, I've found it very difficult to politely say no. That is ... until last week.

"Mr. Crownover," the voice on the phone began, "this is John from Carpets-R-Us, and I would like a couple of minutes of your time to tell you about a special offer that could save you a great deal of money and have your carpets cleaned at the same time."

"John," I answered, "you surely can have two minutes of my time if you will only give me two minutes of your time, right now, to tell you how I can save you a great deal of money on your food. You do eat meat, don't you, John?"

The surprised salesman answered a very tentative, "Well, yes."

"Good," I began, "I can make you a special deal on some excellent quality beef, for this week only. Because you have called during this special time, I'm prepared to sell you the highest quality animal for only $.99 per pound and, John, you will have a tough time beating this deal anywhere."

The man laughed a little and said, "Sir, I live in town and don't have any place to keep a cow."

"Not a problem," I continued, "for I will be more than happy to have the beef processed. I will even deliver within a 25-mile radius of my farm, but the processed and delivered price will have to be $1.99 per pound, but still a bargain."

"I'm sorry, sir," John said rather sheepishly, "I'm not the least bit interested in buying any cattle or beef. I called you to try to sell you a carpet cleaning special that we're offering in your neighborhood next week."

"Well, John, if you're not interested in buying my beef, I don't see how I can be interested in purchasing your carpet cleaning services."

"Oh, I get it," the brilliant man concluded, "you're just using this to get rid of me."

"Not at all," I continued. "As a matter of fact, could I have your home phone number so I can contact you the next time I run this special offer for beef?"

A "click" on the other end of the phone was all I heard. How rude of this man to just hang up on me.

Bob

WE HAVE A HORDE of squirrels that live in the trees in our yard. Large oaks, a walnut and several persimmon trees provide both food and shelter to these little animals that would have to travel at least a quarter mile to find other cover. As a result, I find a great deal of amusement in watching the critters while I sit and drink my morning coffee (I've always heard that older people enjoy watching wildlife).

"Last year, there was a pretty good crop of acorns, walnuts and persimmons available to the squirrels. All autumn long of '95, I watched the squirrels gathering and storing the nuts and persimmon seeds in their homes high atop the trees. All but one worked diligently to store enough food to get them through the winter. One little squirrel that I named Bob, because he had short ears, never joined in the work. Bob was always playing instead of working. He would run along the wooden rail fence of the yard teasing the dog or constantly trying to get the other squirrels to play with him. Sometimes he would simply sit on a limb, soaking up the autumn sun, while watching the other squirrels hard at work.

When winter finally came that year, I watched Bob go over to his neighbor's hole every day and emerge a little while later with an acorn or persimmon seed. He wasn't as fat as the rest of the squirrels, but he made it through the winter on the charity of his neighbors.

This past fall there wasn't nearly as much food for the squirrels to gather. A dry summer had shortened the supply of nuts and seeds, so the other squirrels worked even harder and faster to gather what there was to be had. Bob still enjoyed teasing the dog and watching his friends do all the work. He seemed to enjoy life more than the others.

The first really cold snap this winter found Bob going over to the same hole he received handouts from last winter. But this time Bob and I were both surprised to see the neighbor squirrel running him away. I guess there wasn't enough food in his own den to provide charity this winter.

During the second cold snap this winter, I was saddened to see Bob lying beneath the oak tree of his home ... dead. The dog that he had teased for two years was not nearly as sad as me. He ate Bob.

Animal Rights People

I WAS REALLY DISAPPOINTED this past weekend. A couple of inches of snow and the coldest temperatures we've had in the past three winters required me to spend most of my weekend chopping ice on the ponds and hauling hay to hungry cattle. But that's not why I'm so disappointed.

I'm disappointed because none of the animal-rights people showed up on a below-zero morning to either help me out or to protest my interference with the "natural state" of the animals. Last summer at the fair, these people protested against our keeping the beasts tied up. Never mind that they were fed the best feeds, washed daily, kept under a fan at all times and picked up after. So I assumed they cared so much about the animals that when the water froze over, they would be the first around to help out or, if they disagreed, they would at least protest against the chopping of ice. Either way, I expected to see them. I suspect it might have been more inconvenient on an icy day in December with no one from the media around than it was on an 80-degree day at the fair with lots of media present.

I'm reminded of a meeting held in Wyoming a few years ago as the animal-rights people protested the use of the steel-jawed trap to help control the coyote problem in the middle of sheep country. Both animal-rights groups and ranchers had been invited to a town meeting to try to come to terms on what could solve the problems that both sides claimed they had.

As the meeting prolonged, a lady from the animal-rights group stood up and said, "I think I have a solution that both sides can agree upon."

"Marvelous," said the moderator of the meeting, "let's hear it."

"Well," began the lady, "my group would be willing to donate all the live-traps we need to trap the coyotes." She continued, "We could then castrate all the males we capture, release them back into the wild, and over time the problem will be solved."

A grizzled old rancher in the back of the meeting room slowly stood up to speak. "Ma'am," he drawled, "you just don't understand. The coyotes ain't a rapin' our sheep, they're a eatin' 'em."

I doubt that we will ever find common ground.

Halbert

THE OPENING OF BIRD SEASON is one of the biggest days of the year for the outdoor sportsman. Before children and career eliminated most of my idle time, the opening of quail season was a much anticipated event in my life.

Walking the open fields on an icy-cold morning, watching a well-trained dog lock up on a covey and nervously waiting for a dozen miniature explosions to fly up and off in at least ten different directions is pure heaven for the bird hunter; it has been my observation that no other type of hunter takes more pride in the art of hunting.

Most of the bird hunters I've ever hunted with would rank at the top in hunter etiquette, safety and sportsmanship. These hunters would rarely take more than their limit, and they would even plug the ammo capacity of their gun to give the birds every sporting chance possible. Those who didn't abide by the rules weren't very welcome in the elite fraternity of bird hunting.

And then there was Halbert.

Back in 1978, I was teaching high school in Carthage, Missouri. The quail hunting was as good as it could get. There were three of us. We went hunting every weekend and sometimes twice or three times during the week. I had invited my good friend, Halbert Smith, to come over for a weekend of hunting. Halbert showed up on Friday night, and we immediately started talking about our dogs and our guns.

"What kind of gun are you going to use tomorrow?" I asked.

Halbert stunned us by saying, "Oh, I brought my 22."

"You can't use a 22 to bird hunt," I laughed.

Halbert just smiled said, "Well, you sure don't need a 30-30 to kill a little bird."

The next morning at the crack of dawn, there were four of us out along a field border with two dogs. One of the dogs was simply too active and had already busted the first covey before we could get to them. Now they began to work the singles. I looked to my left and saw Halbert (who really did have a shotgun) aiming at the ground ahead at one of the single birds that was running along a cow path.

"You're not going to shoot the bird while it's running, are you?" I hollered.

"I am if it doesn't stop first," he replied.

Needless to say, we never found enough of that bird to clean.

Have a Nice Day

THE LITTLE PLEASURES IN LIFE are, many times, the ones that give us the greatest satisfaction. Such was the case for me this past summer as I hauled a load of cattle to the local auction barn.

In July, I decided to go ahead and sell last fall's calves at low feeder calf prices as opposed to keeping them, feeding high-priced grain and selling them later at low-priced heavier weights. Rounding up and loading stubborn cattle in the steamy Missouri heat usually ranks right up there with a root canal or listening to a politician, and since I sell at an evening sale, gathering the cattle in the heat of the afternoon is especially challenging. That Tuesday afternoon in July was no exception; yet after battling the critters for only an hour, I was off to the auction with a trailer loaded with three tons of beef-on-the-hoof.

Even though the sale barn is only 30 miles from my farm, its location requires me to go through the city during the height of the afternoon rush hour, and it is obvious that most city drivers have never pulled a gooseneck cattle trailer. They mistakenly think that pickups, pulling these trailers, can stop on a dime, change lanes at the drop of a hat, and accelerate alongside Dale Earnhart. They are wrong on all counts.

As I pulled onto the busiest street in the city, slowly picking up speed, a sporty convertible abruptly pulled out of a parking lot on my right and directly in front of me. I slammed on the brakes, which sent all three tons of cattle to the front of the trailer. Talking on his cellular phone the driver was oblivious to the problem he had just caused. We hadn't gone 500 feet, however, before a minor accident caused his lane to be blocked. Just as the signal ahead turned red, I quickly checked my mirror and pulled into the left lane. I could have pulled up another three or four car lengths to the signal, but I chose to stop so that my trailer was directly beside the shiny convertible with the sharply dressed man — still talking on his cell phone.

The cattle in my trailer began to do what nervous cattle do after they've been slammed to the front of a trailer. At first, this man in the crisp, white shirt and flashy suspenders was too busy talking on the phone to notice the droplets of cattle waste landing on the hood of his car, but after no more than a minute, his face turned as white as his neatly starched shirt.

Luckily, the light turned green and I took off for the sale barn while my new friend was still stuck in traffic behind the accident. I could see his dramatic gestures and hear his colorful comments out of my open window, but I just tipped my hat, smiled and mouthed, "Have a nice day."

After the calves sold that evening and I proceeded to the cashier's window, I was sure that the other cattlemen were wondering why I was smiling. Neither they nor I had made any money on the cattle sold that evening, but at least I had the satisfaction of knowing that I had taught one person some proper highway manners for dealing with a farm truck and trailer. And ... in my dreams ... I can always imagine that he was some big corporate executive from one of the meat packers, and will get those same cattle someday.

Somethin' for Nothin'

A GOOD FRIEND (I'll call him Lester, just in case the IRS happens to read this) stopped by the other day to share with me his plans for financing the construction of a new swimming pool at his farm. It seems that Lester's wife is dead-set on getting a new pool at their place in lieu of not being able to take a vacation for the past ten years. The price tag of the small in-ground pool is $9,000.

Lester is a cattleman, too, which means he probably didn't make anything close to $9,000 last year. But Lester is a good husband and father; therefore he is pulling out all the stops in order to please his family.

Here is his plan.

Lester's pool will be located in his back yard, a mere ten feet from a cow pasture. His plan is to install a freeze-proof water tank just across the fence, tap into the pool as a water source, and bill the government for 50% of the price tag for cost-sharing the "pond" construction, a la Jed Clampett's cement pond. But even that bold move leaves the cost at a still whopping $4500. Lester also plans to expense the other half as a legitimate farm expense for livestock watering. Being in the 28% tax bracket, Lester plans on getting a $1260 tax break on this year's taxes. That move brings the cost down to only $3240, still $3200 more than he can afford.

With the wellhouse, well and pump now a source of livestock water, it seemed fair to Lester that he should be able to put the cost of those three big-ticket items on a depreciation schedule, thereby reducing his tax bill another $2000. The question remained, what to do with the last $1240 in expenses?

After hours of careful study and number-crunching, Lester calculated the landscaping of the pool (soil conservation expense), water chlorination (ground water decontamination expense) and weekly pool cleaning (equipment repair and maintenance expense) to be exactly $1240.

"What d'ya think?" he asked after an in-depth explanation of his plan. "Those big corporations ain't the only ones who can figure out how to get somethin' for nothin', are they?"

"Why don't you stock it with fish from the Conservation Department, get them to pitch in on the cost as a wildlife habitat, and actually make some money on this deal?" I asked.

"I'm not a greedy person, I only want what is fair," Lester snapped back.

If Lester is successful in this venture, I'm afraid my wife will want me to do the same. Even though I'm sure that equally outlandish projects have been accomplished, my luck would most certainly assure that Lester and I would share a poolside room somewhere ... like maybe Leavenworth.

Gambling

THIS PAST WEEKEND, I took a trip back in time. Not really, but for all the differences in culture and society, it was similar to being in a small town in the Ozarks in the 1950s.

A friend of a friend had told me about this small town on the Kentucky/West Virginia line that had a small livestock auction where cows were cheaper than any other place in the country. Always looking for a bargain, I took off last Friday morning for a 700-mile adventure.

I pulled into this small town around 5:30 P.M. and found the parking lot at the sale barn full of caged chickens, ponies tied to car bumpers, goats in the open trunks of cars and a pot-bellied pig roaming free in between the cars and trucks. The locals were beginning to bring their livestock in for the evening sale in pickups and ton-trucks with home-made racks ... some with just gates wired together to make the racks. The sale barn didn't even have a place for trailers to load and unload. There were only old-style loading chutes.

I checked in at the office to see if they needed to call my bank to ensure that my check would be good later that evening. The owner said, "If you had enough money to get here from Missouri, I reckon you got enough to buy some cattle." He never called my bank.

The sale started promptly at 7:30 P.M. There were at least 400 people crammed into the tiny sale ring that seated only 200, making me realize that this was the social event of the week in this tiny Appalachian mountain town. Being in tobacco country, everyone was smoking, chewing, or both. The arena looked like it must be on fire. I had to stand on the bleacher stairs beside a man who reeked of whiskey and wanted to know what I thought of every animal that sold. Four old men (with three teeth between them) sat in the seats on my other side. They were very friendly and nodded as I took my place. In front of me, sitting on the top rail, was a fat guy with at least six inches of butt-crack exposed. The inside of the ring was lined with people, and as the animals exited the ring, the audience formed the human fence to get them back to their pens. Three ponies sold first, then 18 goats. Five pigs (including the pot-bellied pig that brought $6) and two cages of chickens rounded out the preliminaries before the cattle started selling.

Since there were no scales in the barn, everything sold by the head. The auctioneer was easy enough to follow, since he really didn't chant as much as he simply asked, "Who'll give me fifty, now fifty-five, now sixty ..." The cattle were extremely poor quality, but they **were** cheap. I bought every cow at the sale that I thought strong enough to make the trip back to Missouri. If they live, I'll probably make a little money on them, but even if they don't, the experience was pretty cheap entertainment. I've only been to Vegas once, but no floor show there ever came close to the show at the sale barn at Catlettsburg, Kentucky.

Selling

WHEN YOU CONSIDER all the industries in America, farmers have the most unique way of selling their product: we allow the buyer to set the price for our goods. Beef producers take their calves to the auction and let buyers bid for immediate ownership. Milk producers take whatever price the milk company decides to give that particular week. Grain producers haul a load to the local elevator and sell it based on what the buyer has on the tote board at that precise moment. This method, however workable, is completely opposite of how the rest of the American economy operates ... where the seller sets the price he wants for his goods or service.

Unlike many of my friends, I happen to think this is the best way to do business and wish that other segments of our economy would follow suit. I would like to see a time when a major manufacturer of tennis shoes would haul in a trailer truck load of sneakers to the "shoe auction." After eight dozen pairs of size 10D, black-and-white high-tops sell, the price would begin to drop until one buyer would ask that one of the pairs he has just purchased be split off and resold because it had a bad lace that he had just noticed. The poor-laced shoes would then be sold by the pound for less than they cost to manufacture.

This would be a time when a person drives his truck down to the local furniture store and informs the owner to load up a particular dining room set. However, the thrifty buyer would only be able to pay $300 for the $400 set because of that nasty seasonal production glut of oak dining room furniture and the over-supply it has created. The furniture owner would grimace, but would go ahead and load it.

What a time it would be when the local department store delivery truck, loaded with tires and batteries would pull into my driveway and up to the barn where he could read the price

I'm paying for 16" tires. He must sell them to me for ten dollars each, because he just wouldn't want to haul them back to the store. Fortunately, for me, he would need the money today so he could make a down payment on next year's inventory.

I think I'll call my insurance agent first thing tomorrow morning and let him know that, due to unforeseen good health, my rates will have to be decreased 20% this year.

Classifieds

THE CLASSIFIED ADS HAVE ALWAYS BEEN a great way for farmers to buy and sell an assortment of products and services. There are always "bargains" to be found, but sometimes the message gets lost between what the seller had in mind, and what the prospective buyer reads (or interprets) in the ad.

My own collection of memorable ads includes "Entire dairy herd for sale, A1 bulls used for many years." I'm sure the bulls were A-one, but I suspect they were AI bulls, suggesting artificial insemination. Another ad read, "Alice Chalmers for sale with wide front end." Every "Alice" I have known tended to have a rather wide rear end, but I'm sure the corporate heads at Allis Chalmers were not amused.

"I've also seen "guilt for sale — very cheap." My guilt has always been more expensive, but I know that gilts (young, female hogs) can cost very little. One of my favorites, though, is "Semen tall bull for sale — $1000." I hope they meant Simmental, for a bull as tall as semen would be a little shaver, at best.

Sometimes the ad can read exactly like the seller intended, but can be misinterpreted by a reader who doesn't understand the "lingo." Only two weeks ago I placed an ad in the local paper that was printed the precise way I wanted: "Good, six-foot, brush-hog, priced to sell." I thought this was the shortest, cheapest and best way to describe what I had for sale. Most of the calls inquired about the price, brand name, and whether it was a three-point or pull-type brush hog — but one call was much more interesting.

"I've just moved to the area from Chicago," the voice on the other end began, "and I've bought a few acres south of town. The place is covered with small brush, and I need to get rid of it, but I don't want to use poison."

Sensing a sale, I proceeded with my pitch that would have made a telemarketer envious, when the phone conversation took an awkward turn.

"A six-foot one is pretty big, isn't it?" he questioned.

"Not really," I answered, "it's about the size most small landowners use."

"I don't know if my fences would keep it in. My neighbor says goats are probably better on brush than hogs, anyway."

"Sir," I injected, "this is a tractor-operated, rotary cutter."

"Oh, never mind." Click.

He hung up before I could tell him where he could have found a cheap guilt — I mean gilt.

Dieting

THERE HAVE SURELY BEEN 10,000 diet programs developed over the past quarter century as America becomes obsessed with its collective weight. All promise quick weight loss with little effort. None, as far as I know, have delivered on the promises — until now. Last week, quite by accident, I discovered a quick, easy and effective way to realize tremendous weight loss.

Eight years ago, I bought my first cab tractor. My wife thought it would be best for the safety of the children, and the salesman was very insistent as well. "You will need an air conditioner on this model," he said.

"I don't think so," I stated, since it just seemed like an unnecessary expense to me.

"Have you ever driven a cab tractor, in the summertime, without air conditioning?" he asked.

"I haven't ever driven a cab tractor, period," I responded.

He eventually persuaded me of the necessity, so I purchased the tractor — air conditioning and all. Until last week, I have still never driven a cab tractor without air when, at the height of hay season, the air conditioning finally gave up the ghost. Being too busy cutting, raking and baling hay to take it to a mechanic, I made hay all week in what can only be described as a "greenhouse" on wheels. With a cab equipped with 128 square feet of glass (I measured it), the temperatures inside were well over 110 degrees most afternoons, even with the windows open their maximum four inches (no doubt an OSHA requirement to keep small children and distraught farmers from jumping to their death).

I started the week at a top weight of 215 pounds. Today, only six days later, I am a trim 195, having trouble keeping my pants up. This is a major weight loss breakthrough. Now all I need is some fat celebrity to go through my program, get on TV and tell how successful it is, and I'll be a rich man in no time. I might even turn my cattle farm into a "fat farm" for famous people to come and shed those ugly pounds.

I think I'll write Oprah and see if she is interested. Considering what she's done for the beef industry lately, locking her in the cab of a tractor on a hot day seems like the least I could do.

Boredom

HAULING ROUND BALES from the field to the bale yard has to be one of the most boring and monotonous jobs a farmer must endure. Back and forth, over and over, one bale at a time for hours upon hours starts a man to thinking, "Can this career choice really be worth it?" Retrieving the bales also proves an interesting phenomenon of farming — the heaviest producing part of the hayfield will always be the farthest point from the bale yard.

Such were my thoughts last week as I began the task I had put off for as long as I possibly could. I don't know whether it was the heat (I still don't have the tractor air conditioner repaired) or the boredom that led me to question whether anyone in America had a more trivial job than this ... until I happened to remember a workshop I attended last winter.

At this winter workshop on intensive grazing systems, I listened intently to quite an interesting presentation on how to manage twice as many cattle on the same number of acres by fencing and rotating small areas of pasture. I was learning a lot and becoming very interested in installing this system on my farm when, suddenly, the workshop led to the side benefits of manure distribution. The speaker offered chart after chart after colorful chart, describing the number of "cow piles" per square yard, the average distance of the piles from the water source, and the weight of the manure per acre (complete with fertilizer nutrient breakdown). While the rest of the audience was engrossed in these facts, all I could think about was, "Who sat there and watched all these cows defecate, then measured the distances and weighed the piles to compile all this data?"

I could only assume some lowly graduate student, trying their best to please their major professor and get enough usable data to publish a thesis, was sitting under a shade tree with a clipboard. I could also imagine this graduate student coming home at night and his spouse asking him, "Honey, how was your day?"

The response must have been, "I sat ... for eight hours ... and watched cows crap."

Hauling round bales doesn't seem so bad after all.

Cowboys

IF YOU COULDN'T TELL a real cowboy from a wannabe by his independent nature, then you surely could by looking at the pickup he drives. My neighbor is a good example, both in attitude and vehicular transportation.

Joe Bill (I'll use this assumed name, since court proceedings are still pending as I write this story) runs a couple of hundred momma cows up the road a piece from my place. His pickup truck is a mid-to-late seventies Chevy. The doors are each a different color, but it doesn't matter, since neither match the color of the primer gray hood or the rust-colored, once-white body. It's a three-quarter ton, four-wheel drive, log wagon that seats two if you can move enough syringes, ropes, overshoes, pop cans and baler twine to utilize the passenger's side. The truck was washed once, back in the early eighties, and runs amazingly well except when it has to idle for long periods of time.

With an estimated worth of $800 on the pickup, I was a bit surprised when Joe Bill drove by one day with a brand new, $5000, state-of-the-art, hydraulic bale bed and unroller attached to this heap of junk. You see, in my part of the country, real cowboys have these types of beds on their trucks. And let there be no mistake — Joe Bill is a real cowboy.

Everything seemed to be going smooth for Joe Bill this winter. Feeding hay was much easier with his new gadget, and the truck ran as if it would make it another 20 years, except for the few times when he would forget and let it idle for ten minutes while he tagged a new calf or stopped on the road to visit with a neighbor. For some reason, this caused the truck to die in its tracks, and nothing would make it start until the engine cooled.

Joe Bill's good fortune turned sour one Friday afternoon in Springfield, Missouri. In town for his monthly supplies, Joe

Bill found himself in bumper-to-bumper traffic on Glenstone Avenue. For those of you who have never been on Glenstone during Friday afternoon rush hour traffic, it is quite simply 10,000 cars moving at the speed of a small glacier.

Traffic jams, blaring horns, obscene gestures and a cowboy with an attitude do not mix very well. As Joe Bill was idling along at 2 mph, he was followed by a little blue-haired woman in a Lincoln Continental, whose horn worked very well. Joe Bill felt the old Chevy begin to lose power and tried to change lanes so he could pull off before it died. But changing lanes was impossible for anyone that afternoon, much less Joe Bill. The truck died on the inside lane, 200 yards short of the next stop light.

Joe Bill was stuck, and so were the scores of cars and trucks behind him. The little blue-haired woman in the Continental began to honk. And honk. And honk. Joe Bill was mad at the truck and everyone who couldn't understand his predicament. The woman was still honking.

Joe Bill could stand it no more. After cranking on the engine for what seemed like five minutes, he turned the key to "Accessory." Grabbing the controls for the bale arms, he started raising them from the stationary position. Slowly the arms raised, until they were straight up. Down the arms came, more rapidly now, until they creased the fenders of the Lincoln Continental (the manufacturers of the bale bed probably didn't take this into consideration during the design phase). Joe Bill continued to lower the arms until they were even with the lady's wheels. The arms constricted until they grabbed the wheels. Joe Bill then raised the arms — and the Continental — until both were about three feet off the ground. He cranked the window down, stuck his head out, and looked square at the woman. "Give 'er hell, lady, 'cause you're the one drivin' now."

If the little blue-haired woman hadn't figured out from the truck that Joe Bill was a cowboy, she surely did from his attitude.

Tractors

IN 1952 MY FATHER BOUGHT his first, last and only new tractor — an 8N Ford. He paid $500 for the tractor (a great deal of money in 1952), and it faithfully served him for the remainder of his life and farming career.

Today the tractor has thousands of hours on an engine that has been completely overhauled three separate times. It sits in my barn as one of my most cherished possessions. It still runs good, is capable of performing many of the smaller chores on the farm, and is worth about six times what it cost new, some 46 years ago.

Last week, I traded for a new tractor — partly because I needed a bigger tractor, partly because I was tired of the ribbing from my friends and neighbors for owning a "foreign tractor," but mostly because I wanted the same brand that had served my dad so well.

When it was delivered last Thursday, everyone in the family was impressed. I was like a kid with a new toy; my sons even had an argument over which one would get to do the bush-hogging and bale-moving this summer (thank you, Lord), and even my wife thought it was an "attractive" tractor until she asked the eventual question, "How much did it cost?"

Even though my good friends over at S&H Farm Supply had given me a great deal on the tractor, when I told my wife the cost, I considered calling 911. She became pale, sweaty and shaky. I went and got her a glass of water.

"You paid HOW MUCH?" she continued.

"Think of it as an investment," I said. "Remember Dad's 8N? It's worth six times what he gave for it 40 years ago."

Judy chose her words carefully as she responded, "So what you're telling me is that 40 years from now, that tractor will be worth $200,000. That's your story?"

"Based on historical data, the present-day economic climate

and current machinery appreciation trends, yes," I replied rather sheepishly. It was beginning to look like I might have to spend a few nights sleeping in the comfortable cab of the new tractor.

"That's some story," she said as she walked away.

So, in the words of that famous country-western song, "That's my story and I'm stickin' to it." I would also appreciate it greatly if my friends and neighbors would stick to the same story if Judy asks them about my "investment." I would be forever grateful.

Cheap

AT THE PRESENT TIME, anyone in Missouri who is involved in agriculture knows how cheap live cattle are. We haven't seen cattle this cheap in many years and, hopefully, when it does turn around, we won't see it this bad for many more years to come.

Last Sunday I got a phone call from a good friend of mine who lives in eastern Nebraska and owns a cattle feedlot there. The story he told me certainly illustrates just how bad things are in the beef business these days. He swears this actually happened only a few weeks ago at a sale barn a few miles west of his feedlot.

On sale day, a local dairy farmer brought eight Holstein baby calves to the auction barn. The first calf into the ring didn't even get a bid. The second calf came in and also received no bid. After the third calf came in and failed to get even a tap of the nose, the owner stood up slowly and said, "I know cattle are cheap right now, and you might have to spend more on feed than you could get out of the calves, but if anyone is interested in taking these eight calves home, then I'll just give them to you free."

"Well, if you're going to make that kind of offer, I guess I would take them for free," replied another local farmer. "But I'll have to go back to the farm and get my trailer," he added, making sure everyone knew he had no intentions of buying cattle that day.

Pitiful as it is, this should have been the end of the story. However, when the farmer returned for his free calves, there were 12 calves waiting in the pen instead of eight. Apparently someone else had found a quick way to get rid of some unwanted calves.

Heat

THERE ARE SOME WEEKS when I really struggle to come up with real-life illustrations for just how simple life really is. And then ... there are weeks, like this last one, where it is handed to me on a silver platter.

Second semester classes started on Tuesday at the University. The building in which I teach has an absolutely terrible heating and cooling system, so when we get an unusually warm winter day, like last Wednesday, some rooms become uncomfortably hot because you can't regulate the heat properly. The classroom where I teach is one of the worst at becoming too hot.

In between two of my classes, a professor from another department (I won't mention the name of that other department) teaches a class in this "hot" classroom. Immediately after class, this professor stormed into my boss's office, losing her temper while complaining about how miserable it was in her classroom. She rudely whined that it was "as hot as a sauna," "impossible to teach" and several other descriptions that are too explicit to mention.

My boss found me and told me what had just happened and asked if it was really that hot in the room or if this lady with a Ph.D. was over-exaggerating the situation.

"Yes," I replied, "it really was too hot when I first went in, but after we opened a window for just a few minutes, it was very comfortable."

Jumping the Fence

MANY YEARS AGO, our neighbor had a bull that wouldn't stay home. I'm certain that the sorry-excuse-for-a-fence that separated the neighbor's land from ours was a major contributing factor to the frequent visits, but the bull also seemed to have more than the necessary amount of testosterone in his system. The bull could smell a cow in heat for three miles in any direction and could get to the cow regardless of the amount of brush, number of fences, depth of creek water, or steepness of cliffs that separated the amorous bovines. He was on a mission.

Strangely enough, after the bull had completed his "mission," he would return to his home farm. It was a rare event to catch the sly critter in the act or even close to the scene of the crime. Even though our cows produced calves, year after year, that were obvious genetic proof of the bull's trespass, his owner denied that his bull would do such a thing. Confronted with the offspring of our cows, he always stuck by his story of denial ... denial ... denial.

We put up with these transgressions until the bull visited a group of young heifers that were *too* young to begin their motherhood. Enough was enough. Since I was young enough that my labor wouldn't be missed for a few days, but old enough to handle the double-barreled shotgun, I was assigned to "guard" the heifers.

"Aim high from about 30 yards," my dad instructed me, "we don't want to kill him, just teach him a lesson."

For three days I routinely watched the herd of heifers. On the fourth day the visitor arrived: snorting, bellowing and sniffing the air. Hidden in the fence row, I raised the weapon and gently cocked both barrels of the shotgun loaded with bird shot. As I took aim over the top of the bull as my father had instructed me, I realized that the bull's problem of "over-affection" originated somewhat lower in his anatomy (being a farm boy, I understood these things even at the tender age of 11). Standing directly behind the bull at about 30 yards, I lowered my aim and squeezed one trigger. After the noise of the shotgun subsided, the sounds of the bull echoed for miles as he ran toward his home. Fortunately, the bull never came back to our farm. Unfortunately, my aim was better than I thought, and he never sired any more calves for his owner either.

Given the similarity between our neighbor's bull of 35 years ago and some modern-day politicians, I suspect that some of these politicians' wives would like to borrow the old double-barreled shotgun to help solve the problem of their husbands "jumping the fence."

They just need to remember the instructions — shoot high if you want to scare them, but shoot low if you want to solve the problem.

Warmth

It took several layers of clothing to stay warm while feeding the cattle during this last cold spell. Farmers and ranchers have long known how to dress in order to keep from freezing with prolonged exposure to frigid temperatures. My buddy, Gary, was a master at dressing warm.

I worked for Gary and his brother on their ranch in between my stint as a high school agriculture teacher and college professor. They ran several hundred head of cattle, so winter feeding was an "all-day-long" adventure. With no time to come in and warm yourself during the day, you had to be dressed for the weather when you left at 7 A.M., and remain that way until early evening.

One exceptionally cold day in January of that year, knowing that we would encounter frozen water pipes, pond ice thick enough to drive over and a northwest wind that would cut through you like a knife, we dressed with even more layers than normal that morning. When we eventually got back to the house, around 6 P.M. that evening, we started to unwrap ourselves in the mudroom of the house, anticipating the roaring wood fire that awaited us inside the home. Gary started taking off his coat, vest, insulated overalls, jeans, long-handled underwear and, to my startled eyes ... pantyhose!

I was already running as fast as I could toward the nearest door when he yelled, "Whoa ... what's wrong?"

I carefully stuck my head back through the door opening, keeping a strong grip on the doorknob, and replied, "I had no idea you were ... er ... a ..." Gary stopped me in mid-sentence.

"I am not," he answered curtly, "it's just that these really keep you warm on a day like today."

I didn't doubt his word, since he had never lied to me

before, but I never had the guts to verify it for myself. To this very day, I still wonder though, how he found pantyhose big enough to fit a 6'4", 240-lb. man. I didn't ask ... and he didn't tell. A pretty good policy after all.

Dad

My father lost his battle with cancer this past week. I had tried my best to remain strong throughout this past year, because that's the way Dad had raised my sisters and me — to accept what you couldn't change, without shedding any tears. He had lived his life as a compassionate, yet strong man, who seldom showed his emotions in a manner that other people could see. Always wanting to be like my dad, I had refused to cry.

Five days before Dad passed away, it was snowy and cold. After leaving work early to come home and help my mother and sisters care for him, I left his side for an hour or so to feed the cattle. The chores had become a more hurried routine of late, so I could get back as quickly as possible and help with Dad. I was at the rented farm, a mile from our home, when I noticed that a recently purchased cow had calved an hour or so before I got there. The baby calf was still wet and was shivering from the cold snow that was falling. I quickly put out hay for the cows and immediately drove out of the field, hoping that the calf would make it in this weather.

I had already closed and chained the gate when I realized that my father would never leave a wet and cold newborn calf to "make it" on its own. I unlocked the gate, drove back to the barn and walked out in the woods to the calf. Picking up the calf, I carried it about 200 yards to the warmth of the barn and placed it on some dry bedding. The cow followed and both were sheltered for the night.

As I left the field for the second time, I felt good knowing that I had done what my father had taught me his entire life. He had always taught me by example instead of constantly telling me what to do. Evidently he had been successful.

I locked the gate behind me, got in the truck, and then ... I cried.

Thanks, Dad, and goodbye.